YOU WANT TO BE AN ENTREPRENEUR

Success requires more than a great idea

by

Jeff Stoller
JD, MBA, MBT

Published by 321 Bayshore Investments, Inc.
1717 N Bayshore Drive, Penthouse A56
Miami, FL 33132 USA 1-866-653-4245
info@321bayshoreinvestments.com

1st edition June 2015

YOU WANT TO BE AN ENTREPRENEUR
By
Jeff Stoller

I.   INTRODUCTION

Each year, tens of thousands of people all over the world set out on a dream to start their own businesses. It is this drive that leads so many of us to leave jobs, to give up security and forego so-called *traditional* paths. While many fail, it is the success stories like the thingamajig that someone made in his or her kitchen that sold 1 million units, or the app that someone thought of in the shower that was sold for millions that motivate us each day.

Most entrepreneurs fall into one of a few categories:

- They may be sales people who believe they've found the hottest thing in the country or just think they can do better on their own than by working under or with someone else.

- They may be inventors who believe they've invented the "better mouse trap."

- They may simply be bored with whatever they've been doing, whether it's been as an attorney or a housewife, and are looking for something more fulfilling.

- Then there are those people who have had an idea forever and just didn't know how to go about doing it.

For all the reasons to start one's own business, these people should be congratulated. Why, though, do so many fail? The answer is that something was missing from the equation that makes a business successful. The missing element could have been a proper evaluation of the merits of the idea or location, a realistic assessment of the skills or personality of the principal(s), adequate capital, adequate knowledge of the market, good staffing and others. Or, it could be something that has nothing to do with the entrepreneur and over which the entrepreneur had no control – there is such a thing as bad timing and bad luck.

There are hundreds if not thousands of books about business – general views, specific views, opinions about this, statistics about that. So, why should you read this book?

Before answering that question, it is relevant to know something about me. I am an attorney, accountant, consultant and professor. I am also an entrepreneur. I have started my own businesses. I have succeeded and I have failed. The advice in this book is not coming from someone who has never actually done it or a pure academician, but rather someone who has seen it from all sides. Sometimes when we get advice, especially from a professional, our gut response is "He doesn't know what I'm going through, and he's never done it." Consequently, maybe we don't trust the advice or don't give it as much credit as we should. In fairness to many very good attorneys, accountants and consultants, even though they have not done exactly what you are doing, they can still be right. Still, I have been there. I have experienced many of the highs and lows described in this book; and made some of the same mistakes I caution you about.

Back to the question: Why should you read this book?

> Any book that says it has "all the answers" is, to be polite, inaccurate and misleading. No book has all the answers. But this book has a lot of the questions you need to ask and for which you will need answers.

> No author is in exactly your shoes. Your situation, your background, your ideas and your intellect are all unique to you – and what works for you may not work for someone else and vice versa. This book will not tell you how to run your business or get into any specific ideology of how I think you should operate. But this book will give you information and knowledge to help you make those choices for yourself and, if you do get advice from some professionals, you will be able to better understand and evaluate their advice rather than be like some people when we go to the auto mechanic and he or she tells us what's wrong with some widget and we try to look like we know what they are talking about but we're really thinking "whatever."

Consider all the books an undergraduate business or MBA student reads in the course of his or her education... And they still don't have all the answers. (They may think they do when they graduate, but they quickly learn it ain't so.) What those books and courses accomplish is to put the students in a better position to figure out the answers when they are confronted with a specific set of facts. This book is not intended to get you to that same point, but it will give you an advantage over the people who simply charge ahead into the unknown with no clue what they're doing.

As an entrepreneur, it is your inspiration and drive that contribute to the creation and realization of your dream. Your time is better spent developing and implementing your ideas while others can help you with the answers that will aid you in your endeavor.

You should read this book if you would like help to begin the process, to better communicate your ideas to others and to know when there are questions that need to be addressed. You should read this book if you would like some basic information to help you better understand the challenges you will encounter and to recognize situations when you need to ask someone else a question. Since no one can know all the answers, you are at least in a *better* position if you know many of the questions.

Lastly, while this book was written from the point of view of a business in the United States in regard to some of the laws and regulations, the business principles are applicable virtually anywhere and any specific rules mentioned in this book probably have a corollary in whatever country you are reading this.

II.   BEING AN ENTREPRENEUR

A.   INTRODUCTION TO ENTREPRENEURSHIP

1.   Success stories

We've all heard many entrepreneurial success stories; too many to mention. Remember, too, that all major corporations today were once entrepreneurial ventures. McDonald's, Ford Motor Company, IBM, Exxon, American Airlines to name a few were all started by one or just a few people based on an idea and hard work. At a certain point, we stop thinking of a business as "entrepreneurial" because of its size or value, but in every case *someone* had to start it – and that someone was an entrepreneur.

You may have a very different attitude toward those companies when thinking of them as the evolutionary result of an entrepreneurial business.

2.   Non-success stories

Equally important to using the success stories as motivation and inspiration is an understanding of the businesses that don't succeed. Several points need to be made here:

a. Poor management is a key reason for business failures. More money alone would not have made those businesses a success.

b. Improper budgeting and inadequate capitalization (i.e., not enough money to start either because of poor planning or a willingness to start too soon) will kill a business as fast as any bad management decisions. Often, a person wants something so much that he or she will cut corners or "justify" certain things for the purpose of getting something going even though it is destined to fail as a result.

> Example: You invented a new gadget that you can have manufactured for you for $1, and you can sell it for $3; and you have $1000 to buy 1000 gadgets that you can sell for $3,000.

5

Sounds pretty good, right? The problem is that the people who manufacture the gadget for you have to be paid now while the people you sell to will not pay you for 30-90 days. Until you get paid, how do you pay your rent, phone, Internet, or buy food, support your family and buy more gadgets to fill orders? How many times have you watched Shark Tank and heard the entrepreneurs say they need the money to fill orders that they cannot deliver? But that alone is almost never enough because the business also needs capital to cover the operating expenses between the time your customer pays for the goods and when they receive payment for the goods they shipped.

c. IF A BUSINESS DOES NOT SUCCEED, IT DOES NOT MEAN THE ENTREPRENEUR IS A FAILURE. A business may not succeed because of timing, design, location, capital, experience, contracts, etc. If you lack the needed skills or outside factors contribute to the termination of your business, <u>this is not a reflection on your worth as a person</u>. Your friends will still like you, most business associates will understand and your family will still love you. This fear should not be the deterrent to starting a business. If you lack some key requirements for starting a particular business, those are obstacles to overcome or maybe reasons to delay. The fear of being viewed as a failure should not be the reason you don't start a business AND it should not cause you to isolate yourself from your family, friends and even former employers if your business does not succeed.

B.   WHY BE AN ENTREPRENEUR

You can be an entrepreneur for many reasons; sometimes because you want to and sometimes because you have to. One or more of the following may be your reason(s):

- You're unhappy with your job and want to do something else.
- You have an idea that you think will work in the marketplace.
- You're unhappy working for someone else.
- You like what you're doing but think you can do it better.

- You've been laid off and need something to do and some way to support your family.
- You see a gap or something missing in the market and you think you can fill it.
- You just enjoy sitting around coming up with new ideas.

C. WHERE TO START

For some people, the entrepreneurial endeavor is guided by a particular expertise. If you're a rocket engineer, you might create a business in that field of technology. If you're a cook, you might start a restaurant or other food related business.

For other people, it is an idea born out of necessity ("necessity is the mother of invention") regardless of the inventor's previous skills. Whether that necessity is *real* or *imagined* is a different issue.

It makes good sense to start with something within your particular expertise. Most entrepreneurs are surprised and often disappointed how involved they are with aspects of the business unrelated to what they know and enjoy.

For example: A cook who wants to open a restaurant must deal not only with cooking, but also:

- Landlords and leases
- Purchasing and suppliers
- Employees, personnel problems, labor laws
- Building codes and city bureaucrats
- Artists and printers
- Insurance brokers
- Accountants
- Bank and credit card companies.

The story is the same no matter what you want to do. The question is not whether you're smart enough to do each one of these things, because you probably are. The question is whether you have (a) the mental and physical energy to learn all of them fast enough, then do them all and do them well enough, and/or (b) the relationships (maybe others who also believe in your vision) or resources (money to pay others) to have others with more experience than you perform those tasks.

D.   THE PERSONALITY OF THE ENTREPRENEUR

You've probably seen surveys and quizzes about the personality traits of an entrepreneur. *Knowing yourself* is one of the most important elements of being a successful entrepreneur.

For example, if you like stability, security and predictability you may not like being an entrepreneur. If, on the other hand, you have a burning desire to make your mark or be on your own, you may want to try your own business at some point in your life, even if you do it on the side while keeping your regular job.

You might have met entrepreneurs whom you thought were very egotistical and materialistic. In measured doses, these characteristics can contribute to being a successful entrepreneur.

- Without some materialistic drive, you might not be reading this book.

- Without some amount of ego, you might not have the confidence to defy the odds and "go for it." There's a big difference, however, between having an ego and being an egotistical jerk. You can have a big ego, know it and know when you're doing things to satisfy your ego as opposed to any real business need or objective. The egotistical jerk alienates people and surrounds himself or herself with people who do not contribute to the business but only say "Yes" and   compliment (as opposed to *complement*, which is very different) the boss.

E. PLUSES AND MINUSES OF BEING AN ENTREPRENEUR

Being an entrepreneur has many pluses and minuses. HOWEVER YOU PERCEIVE YOURSELF, REMEMBER ALSO THAT BEING AN ENTREPRENEUR AFFECTS THE PEOPLE AND LIVES AROUND YOU - POSITIVELY AND NEGATIVELY. It's a balancing act and involves choices you have to make - maybe with your family - carefully.

1. Potential pluses of being an entrepreneur

a. The feeling of success

Success is wonderful. The feeling of accomplishment, particularly when the odds were against you, is incredible.

b. You're your own boss

No one tells you what to do or how to do it. You're free to do a job the way you want to do it - the same, better or worse than someone else might have.

c. You have control

You have much more control over your destiny (although still not total). If you succeed, you can legitimately take the credit. Though, as a good manager, it's not a good idea to minimize the efforts and contributions of others without whose help the business would not succeed.

d. Family participation

In your own business, you're free to hire whomever you want; and, hopefully, you can trust your family at least as much as anyone else.

A few caveats: Don't make business conflicts personal ones. Don't alienate your spouse and children by talking only about business. Keep the relationship as balanced as possible. Lastly, be careful whom you hire and the responsibilities you assign because it's hard to fire a family member who is either unqualified or taking advantage of the relationship and not doing his or her job.

e.   You can provide your family with something more than just your income

When you work for someone else, your compensation is primarily income. Your savings and investments are what you build for your family. In some cases, this may actually be preferable to owning your own business since you can invest in a variety of things rather than one business. However, by building your own business, you could have a revenue producing vehicle that your family can continue and build.

f.   The opportunity to "leave your mark" that will last longer than you

Some psychologists say that's the same reason we have children - something to indicate "I was here."

g.   Creating an income flow that will last after you stop working

What do a highly paid attorney and a minimum wage clerk have in common? They both are paid by the hour; which means that if either doesn't work, he or she doesn't earn. If either wants to go away for a vacation, not only does it cost whatever the vacation costs but also the earnings lost by not working (unless they have paid vacations). So, the attorney builds a law firm with many other attorneys, bringing in revenues so he or she can keep drawing a salary even when not working. What can the minimum wage clerk do? He or she can be an entrepreneur and, hopefully, a successful entrepreneur.

When you have a job, you make a living and, in some cases, are entitled to a pension when you retire. When you build a business, hopefully the business can support both you and the person you've passed the reins to, and you've got a built-in pension.

h.   The greater the risk, the greater the reward

When the business is yours, you stand to lose the most. You also stand to gain the most. There is almost certainly more risk in being an entrepreneur, so you need the rewards to be greater. This is one of the reasons you must carefully analyze your proposed business because it would be a shame if you started the business and it was as successful as it could be - and you still didn't make more money or enjoy the other advantages of being an entrepreneur.

> Example: John works for a big company now and makes a good salary. He loves to cook and wants to do something on his own. He has an idea for a restaurant and, even if it's successful, will not mean a lot more money than what he's making now. He'll also be working more hours. John also wants to spend more time with his wife and children, who will work with him in the restaurant; and he wants to have something to leave his children and their children. In this case, the potential for the other pluses may compensate for the fact that the short term monetary reward was not as much as would be desired.

2.   Minuses of being an entrepreneur

a.   Instability and insecurity

An entrepreneur who is just starting out often doesn't go to work knowing there's a salary at the end of the week. If an employee makes a mistake, chances are the company will survive and the employee will keep his or her job. If you make a serious mistake in your own small business, that could be the end. On the other hand, one of the reasons many people are starting their own businesses is that they don't feel their jobs are very secure anyway.

b.   Responsibility

In a large organization, functions are specialized and there are many people to rely on, each with his or her expertise. In a small business, people often do multiple functions and much of that responsibility will fall upon you as the entrepreneur. Hopefully, you'll have a few close advisors and associates who can give you their opinions and counsel.

c. Pressure

The combination of your being responsible for so much and the instability of a start-up business creates 24 hour pressure. The pressure can have a dramatic effect on your personality and relationships with family and friends. Some people may become withdrawn, while others may become more outgoing. Some people who have big egos start to believe they know everything and become impossible to talk to, while others fall apart from indecisiveness. The pressure may not affect you, but if you are aware of it, you might recognize it more easily and deal with it sooner if it does happen.

d. Greater family expectations

Family members and sometimes friends may take for granted or presume that you will give them a job. Also, since family members, especially children, may be anticipating going into business with their parents, there is often a feeling of betrayal if you sell the business or even if it fails. This could turn into your resenting them for thinking they have any "rights" with respect to your business; and though this may sound extreme, all too often, it is a reality.

e. Total creative freedom

This sounds like a plus, and it can be; but it is also a minus in the sense that you've got no one else to blame since all decisions are ultimately yours. That's a big burden to carry.

f. You're your own boss

Again, this sound like a plus, and it can be. Some people think this gives you the right to not be there whenever you feel like it. Well, you do have that right; but it usually works out that you're working much more and much harder than anyone else or than you ever worked as an employee. And when you're not working, you're worrying or thinking about the business. When you're a new entrepreneur, you can't work 9-5 and leave your work at the office. There's too much riding on what you're doing. The other minus about being your own boss is that you're the one that's supposed to have all the answers. You don't have anyone to look up to on a day-to-day basis and ask, "What's right?" Try to have someone – not an employee – you can bounce ideas off of, who will be honest with you even if it's something you don't want to hear. Employees will tend to tell you what they think you want to hear; and family members will want to be supportive and may not tell you things that might upset or disappoint you.

g. Risk

You might be giving up a job which represents all or a good part of your household income. You might be agreeing to personally pay some business debts if the business doesn't or can't. You could be taking cash away from you and your family now and for the future. All of these are risks to be considered along with their impact on the people around you and the people who depend on you.

h. Failure

The fear of failure dooms many people to fail right from the start. At the other end are the people who are so oblivious to the possibility of failure that they ignore important details and they, too, fail. Also significant is the psychological impact of failure on people who really worked hard and, for whatever reasons, the business didn't succeed. Sometimes, it takes a long time to become motivated again; but, believe me, it does happen.

If you try your hand at being an entrepreneur and it doesn't work out, do not withdraw from friends and family assuming they will think less of you. Do not even hesitate to go back to your old job (unless you left on bad terms) and be honest, be proud of what you tried to do and, if you want, ask for your old job back. Seriously, this happened to me and I learned this lesson the hard way.

III.   THE BUSINESS PLAN

The following outline is intended to highlight the elements that could be included in a business plan. Not all business plans are alike, and each has its own emphasis and focus. So, some elements may be more important in one business plan than another, and other elements may be less important. This discussion is not all inclusive. You should use common sense and possibly consult a professional in deciding what additional information or materials are appropriate to include.

What is a business plan? A business plan is a document that clarifies in your mind and clearly conveys to others:

(a) what you want to do;

(b) how you plan to do it and what it will take in terms of people, money and other resources; and

(c) what you expect the results to be and why.

A good business plan forces you to think through many of the details of how you get from Point A to Point B. For example, you have an idea for a new widget – and it works great! But how do you make it? How do you let people know about it? How do you physically get it into their hands? All of these questions – and more – are critical ... UNLESS you create something and let someone else take it from there. This is called licensing, and is for a later discussion.

Who is the business plan for? A business plan can be for:

(1) yourself,
(2) your staff, and
(3) your financing sources.

When the plan is written for your financing sources, your natural instinct may be to embellish the business plan because you are, in a very real sense, trying to sell something; namely, an investment or loan for your business. Despite the purpose being to sell something, resist the urge to make it too blatantly a sales document. Stick to facts and opinions supported by reasonable assumptions, but do it in a way that tells a story and holds the reader's interest.

A. INTRODUCTION (SUMMARY)

Your ability to communicate your message quickly can be the difference between success and failure – at any stage of business.

The introduction or summary is your chance to get the reader's attention. This section should include key points from the rest of the plan that your audience will likely think is important. This section can be from 1 to 3 pages long. For financiers, this section may be the only thing they'll read unless you've grabbed their attention so they say, "This could be good."

B. CONCEPT

This is a detailed description of your idea. Again (and this is true for everything in the plan), communicating your message clearly and quickly is critical.

This section should include the following items:

1. What is the business?

2. What are the specific goods or services to be provided?

3. Why will your business succeed?

This last issue can be based on points of differentiation between your business and others or even a market niche that is created by bigger business. For example, some people say the computer market is full; while others say, "Yes, but there are very few companies making X." The market for X may be a "market niche" (specialty) that you might see in the marketplace and can exploit.

C. THE INDUSTRY

In this section you educate the reader and, equally as important, show him/her you understand the business environment in which you will operate.

a.   Market Definition

Define the market - for the industry, in general, and your business.

    (1) Geographic

        (a)   Where does the general market for your type of business exist now and in the future?

        (b)   Where will your business be located, and is there a market for your type of business there?

        (c)   How large an area will your business serve?

    (2) Product/Service

        (a)   What does the industry offer?

        (b)   Are you offering the same or something different?

        (c)   If different, in what way(s)?

    (3) Demographics - Who is your audience? The following are examples of information that could be considered. Not all will necessarily be applicable, and there may be other characteristics that are. In each case that you think is relevant, what difference does the answer make relative to your business? And if it is not relevant, why?

        (a)   Where do they live? Do they have to travel to get your type of service or product and, if yes, how far will they travel?

        (b)   How old are they?

        (c)   What sex are they?

        (d)   What are their occupations?

(e)   What level of education do they have?

(f)   How much money do they make?

(g)   What kind of cars do they drive?

(h)   How many computers, phones, tablets, TV's do they have?

(i)   Who in the household makes the purchase decisions for your type of product or service?

(j)   What religion are they? NOTE: This and some other factors such as ethnicity have nothing to do with discrimination or bias; but it makes sense to understand cultural, ethnic or religious characteristics that could affect how your audience perceives your product or service and how that may impact your business.

(4) Size of the Market

    (a)   What's the annual sales volume in the industry?

    (b)   What's been the trend over the last several years?

    (c)   What's the outlook for the future?

(5) Economic - How much is the industry affected by changing economic trends?

    (a)   How is the industry affected by inflation, recession, interest rate changes, unemployment?

    (b)   How is the industry affected by prospective legislation?

b.   Competition

There is a classic case study used in business schools which shows the importance of knowing who your competition is:

Many years ago, a mid-west freight railroad company was having problems. The owner said to his top managers, "What are the other railroads doing that we're not?" The managers carefully analyzed the question, found some answers and made changes; then they went broke. Why? Because they viewed their competition as other railroads when, in fact, their competition included other *forms of transporting freight*; namely trucks and planes.

Understanding your competition helps you assess the viability and prospects of your idea, gives you clues about what to do or not do in your business and generally lets you know what you're in for. Any investor who sees you don't know this information will turn around and walk right out the door.

A few of the considerations to look at are:

(1) Who are your major competitors (by name)?

(2) How many total competitors are there?

(3) How big are they?

(4) What are their respective market shares?

(5) Are imports or exports a factor?

(6) How easy would it be or how likely is it that they would see what you're doing and, if it's working, copy you?

c.   Points of Differentiation

What are the points of differentiation, if any, between your business and others in the industry? What makes you special? This can be as simple as location, a new product, being first in the market or better service. But you have to know -- for yourself if no one else -- why you think you'll succeed against your competition.

The following includes some suggestions as to how to view your prospects for success.

(1) New product or new use for an old product

(2) Different service

(3) Better or different location

(4) Different approach

(5) New audience

(6) Timing

(7) Pricing

(8) New design

(9) Better warranty

d.   Barriers to Entry

How easy is it to get into your type of business, and what's stopping or will stop others from competing with you? If, for example, you were starting a steel mill with tens of millions of dollars needed to begin, the *barrier to entry* would be very high. If, on the other hand, you were starting a lawn mowing service where the only thing you need is a lawn mower, the barrier would be low and someone else could start to compete with you as soon as others see you succeed. This is a situation you have to understand and for which you must plan.

> Example: After opening a retail store, as soon as you see the store becoming successful, you might take options on the best locations to prevent someone else from copying you and taking those locations themselves. Money and labor are obvious concerns, but even if you don't take a particular course of action, knowing your options will give you an advantage over everyone who doesn't plan or think ahead as well as you do.

D.   MARKETING

a.   What is "marketing"?

"Marketing," a term that is widely misunderstood, is the entire process of presenting a product or service to your audience. While many people think marketing is a function of sales, the opposite is actually true – sales is a function of marketing.

Marketing includes (in no particular order):

(1) Product Development

(2) Product and Package Design

(3) Pricing

(4) Sales

(5) Advertising

(6) Promotion

(7) Warranties and Service Policies

(8) Special Financing

(9) Strategy

Start with an overall policy or marketing strategy. For instance, your overall strategy might be to market an inexpensive product for a very broad audience or to market an expensive item for a very small audience. In each case, virtually every aspect of marketing will differ greatly between the two general strategies. Sometimes, the nature of your product or service will dictate the answer to that question. So, if your service is to help people find expensive sports memorabilia, you have already defined your overall marketing strategy because of who your audience is.

Are you providing something your audience (a) already wants or (b) doesn't yet know it wants? What will it take to get enough people to pay for this? The answers may be the difference between success and failure.

If your plan entails a product or service with which the reader can't immediately identify, your ability to explain why you will be able to convince customers to buy what you're selling may be the most important element of your business plan; especially if you're trying to raise money for your business.

b.   Product/Service Development; Product and Package Design

In the 1950's, the big American car manufacturers made pretty much whatever they wanted ... and buyers accepted it. Volkswagen and other small imported cars, along with the gas crisis in the 1970's, changed that forever. Now all car companies listen very carefully to what buyers want.

There are companies – Apple is an example – which are innovation leaders and not only set design trends but also create new markets, audiences and needs with new products. Still, throughout the design, testing and after-launch process they conduct focus groups, do beta testing and continuously ask for and listen to consumer feedback.

Do not get so attached to your vision that you are unreceptive to other people's ideas and feedback. At the same time, do not assume that people who say everything you are doing is perfect are being 100% honest with you.

c.   Pricing

(1) Do you plan to be the most expensive, least expensive or middle of the road? And what difference will it make in your market appeal, image and/or competitive strength?

(2) What is your price based on and why?

(a)   Competition

(b)   Cost

(c)   What the market will bear (applicable especially to unique items and luxury goods).

d.   Sales

(1) Distribution Channels

How do you plan to get your products and/or services to your audience? The major distribution channels (which, of course, can be used in combination with each other) are:

(a)   Retail - end users come to your store or place of business, and/or you deliver locally from that location.

(b)   Wholesale Distributors - you sell to people who resell the products to retailers or other "middlemen"

(i)   Who are the distributors?

(ii)   Where are they located?

(iii)   How do they operate?

(iv)   Do they handle similar or competitive goods?

(v)   What do they charge?

(vi)   Do you have any existing relationships with such distributors?

(c)   Internet/Mail order - you sell by receiving orders through a website, an app, over the phone or in the mail

(i)   Do you use an intermediary marketplace such as iTunes, Amazon and eBay, or do you rely on your own website and app to generate sales?

(ii)   Do you do the processing and fulfillment (sending the orders out) or do you have an outside service do it?

- Warehousing?

- Shipping?

- Labor?

- Insurance?

(iii) What do outside services cost versus doing it yourself?

(d) Salespeople who go to the customer - do you use your own salespeople, independent sales representatives or distributors?

(i) Your own salespeople work for you under your direction. Among the advantages are control and focus on only your products and services. Among the disadvantages are supervisory responsibility and fixed overhead costs.

(ii) Independent sales representatives do not work for you or under your direction but sell your products or services, possibly along with similar products or services from other companies. You still fulfill the orders from your inventory. Among the advantages are less overhead and, possibly, broader coverage. Among the disadvantages are less control and the fact that you're not the only company represented by a given individual or company.

(iii) Distributors are separate companies that actually buy and warehouse your product and may use any of these channels of distribution themselves. Among the advantages are that you can deal with fewer companies in larger quantities and with fewer headaches. Among the disadvantages are you're more dependent on a few customers, you have no control over how they market or price your products, and you have less direct contact with customers and the marketplace.

(2) Some of the issues that relate to more than one of the above are:

    (a)   What does your competition do?

    (b)   Where will you get sales people?

    (c)   How will you train them?

    (d)   What sales and presentation materials will you provide?

    (e)   What sales and presentation materials will others provide?

    (f)   Compensation is a major strategic area because of the competition for good salespeople. Compensation is also closely related to the drive for salespeople to compete among themselves and with one's own self. Some forms of compensation are:

        (i)   A salary provides security and removes a financial pressure that might hurt a salesperson's effectiveness. The overall pressure to perform and, possibly, meet quotas still exists.

        (ii)   A commission provides an incentive to hustle and do business. Be careful, though, that the business is profitable business and not just business on which the salesperson can earn a commission. REMEMBER: SALES ARE NOT PROFITS.

        (iii)   A draw provides an advance against commissions, thereby removing some basic financial pressure while still compensating someone based on performance.

        (iv)   A salary plus commission covers the salesperson's basic living expenses with a base less than a straight salary, but the commission (less than a straight commission) still gives incentive to achieve.

(v)   Profit sharing focuses the salesperson's attention on not just "doing business" but "doing profitable business" by giving a portion of the business' profits. Since many companies determine profits only annually, profit sharing is generally given in conjunction with another form of regular compensation. In addition, the employee may not want profit sharing because it is based on a number that he/she has no control over since you might spend too much in another area of the business. You might not want to give profit sharing because it potentially opens your books to employees and encourages them to question your expenditures. Nevertheless, it is an excellent way to promote a team effort.

(vi)   Bonuses can be given to employees based on the owner's discretion or some formula designed to take personal relationships out of the picture. As far as bonuses to the owner go, they must be by formula determined at the beginning of the year otherwise they will be viewed as a distribution of profits and taxed at a higher rate than a bonus considered as "earned income."

(vii) Stock in the company can be given as an incentive for long term performance. In addition to the issue about opening your books to employees as described above in (f), this also gives your employees a long term interest in the business and a right to vote as a shareholder; which can be good if they stay but a hassle if they leave and you want the stock back. It is generally a good idea to have a buy back provision in the event the employee leaves. Stock can be awarded at the discretion of the owner or by formula.

(viii) Stock Options give the employee the right to purchase stock in the company for a certain price for a designated period of time. After the stock is purchased, the issues are the same as in (g), except in this case the employee has actually paid the company something for his/her stock. You can also condition the Stock Options on staying with the company for a certain amount of time (called "vesting").

(ix) Phantom Stock is a way of compensating employees as if they owned stock. You figure their year-end bonus based on the value of stock that you would have given. For instance, if you give someone 100 shares of phantom stock, they would be entitled to the same dividend as a shareholder who actually owns 100 shares of the stock would get. In addition to not having to worry about voting rights or buy-backs, the advantage to the company is that these payments are tax deductible, unlike distributions of dividends to shareholders.

(g) How you allocate customers is an issue if you're concerned with possible conflicts between salespeople. A couple of alternatives are

(i) by territory - such as by city, state or region

(ii) by industry

(iii) by type (wholesale vs. retail, for example)

(iv) by size.

e. Advertising & promotion

   (1) Strategy

Since everyone hopes word of mouth will be enough to sustain the business, almost everyone underestimates the need for and expense of advertising. The reasons are:

> (a) We sometimes think of advertising as only TV or newspaper ads by big companies. In fact, advertising is any means by which you get your message out – including ads, websites and banners on the Internet, search engine ads or elevated placement, some social media (e.g., ads on Facebook).

> (b) We think of advertising as a "discretionary" expense, meaning it's not like rent which if you don't pay, you're out of business. Your business may be able to stay open if you don't advertise, but it might not go anywhere; and you might not able to pay those necessary expenses later as a result of not spending this supposedly "discretionary" expense now. It's better to include advertising in your plan and budget and, if things are going well, cut back.

Sometimes, a new business will focus all its ad efforts at the beginning to get enough word of mouth going. Sometimes, you hold back to see what happens first. While word of mouth may, in fact, be excellent, it is not something you can plan or assume will get you going fast enough. Whatever your strategy is, it should be well thought out and carefully planned.

The kind and extent of advertising that your competition has can tell you several things; among them are:

> What media they're using to reach their audiences,

> How much they're spending to reach their media, and

What kinds of messages they're using.

You might find that while your idea is good, the cost of getting your message out is prohibitive. On the other hand, no matter how much advertising your competition does, you might learn what niche is available for you to exploit. You may even be able to use their advertising to help you.

(2) Options.

There are many options in advertising, including promotions. Only after looking at what your competition does and considering your market strategy, including niche, should you consider those alternatives and cost effectiveness of each.

    (a)   Television - probably local or cable

    (b)   Radio - local

    (c)   Newspaper - don't overlook community newspapers

    (d)   Magazine - you can buy regions or random circulation, not just the whole country: and some magazines even let you pick specific demographics

    (e)   Handouts

    (f)   Trade shows

    (g)   Skywriting

    (h)   Whatever else you think of.

(3) Comparative Analysis

    (a)   A commonly used measure of comparison in advertising is "CPM" or "cost per thousand" ("m" means 1000 in roman numerals). The use of this can be seen in the following example:

            If you were told that a local TV ad would cost $1500 and a radio ad $500, you might assume the radio ad is better value. At the time of day each ad would run, the TV station has 100,000 viewers while the radio has 25,000 listeners.

You might think the radio ad is better value because it's 1/3 the price of the TV ad. However, because of the different audience size, you're not comparing apples to apples. How much does it cost on each medium to reach 1,000 people? The TV ad reaches 100,000 people for $1500 for a cpm of $15.00; while the radio ad reaches 25,000 people for $500 and a cpm of $20.00.

NOTE: The figures used in this example are for demonstration purposes only and should not be taken to mean that radio is more expensive than TV. Each case must be examined separately.

If you had $1500 to advertise with and cost effectiveness were the only issue, the TV ad would seem to be the better value. However, you may have only $500.

(b) More important, though, is that there are many other considerations which apply to all of the advertising and promotion options available to you. A few of those considerations follow.

- Is a visual ad more effective than one that is only heard?

- Is it better to have one ad or several less expensive ads?

- What good is a big audience if it's not your audience? In the above example, assume the TV station's viewers are primarily senior citizens while the radio station's listeners are mostly under 25 years old... and you're selling skateboards. If instead of just figuring cpm based on total audience for your business, which the ad appears. For example, an advertiser that wants to be known for quality would not advertise in a publication that is very cheap no matter how good the cpm.

f.   Promotion

Promotions are a form of advertising which generally involve some activity, such as a giveaway, contest, in-store promotion program, or participation in an event (sponsoring a charity softball game, a runner in a race, etc.). Promotional budgets should be analyzed in conjunction with advertising because the bottom line is to convince people to use your product or service.

The same considerations of effectiveness of exposure and type of image created apply to promotions.

g.   Public Relations

Sometimes called "free advertising" because you are not charged by the magazine, newspaper, station, etc., public relations is another vehicle for getting your message across. Whether you have a public relations person (probably an independent consultant) or do it yourself, public relations can be an excellent opportunity if you have something new or an interesting story to tell. It is not, however, free.

Your outlets for PR include news and trade media (TV, newspapers and magazines), social media, blogs, reviewers and an ever increasing array of opportunities. You just have to be creative.

Talk to a professional for advice and a cost estimate. It might be an unnecessary expense at the beginning, but it doesn't cost anything to learn about your options for now and the future.

h.   Special Warranties; Special Financing

Although these could be combined under "Promotions" they are an increasingly common and important device that deserves special consideration.

To all those people who ask why a discussion of warranty and financing is in the marketing section at all, just look at the auto industry as an example.

For years, the car companies and others have been trying to lure buyers by offering better and longer warranties, rebates and low interest loans.

There is, however, a very real cost to this device. Imagine you're offering financing at 9%. If it costs you 10%, this promotion is costing you 1% (10% - 9%) of all the financing do during this promotion. Extended warranties, on the other hand, are a sign of improved quality and confidence in one's product. Especially with respect to a product that is expected to last a long time and for which repair costs can be high, warranties are a critical marketing tool.

E.   MANUFACTURING/LABOR

a. What Is Involved in Manufacturing and Labor

This section describes your sources for the goods and/or services you intend to provide. In an environment where sales prices may be limited by competition, the successful businesses may be those that can deliver comparable products or services at a lower cost with, consequently, a higher profit.

It is important to think these items through and for others to know that you've thought them through, anticipated potential problems and done what you can to guard against such problems.

(1) What goods and/or services do you need to obtain and to provide your goods and services?

(2) Where will you get them?

(3) Have your intended suppliers dealt with your specific goods/services before? If so, for whom?

(4) How will you get your goods and services and what delays or risks are associated (e.g., a ship sinking)?

(5) How much will your goods and services costs and are costs affected by fluctuating dollar values? If so, by how much and can you "hedge" against such fluctuation?

(6) How reliable are your sources? Will you be waiting for an order and the source never manufactured it, never shipped it or shipped it to the wrong place?

(7) How dependent are you on limited or uncertain sources? Do you have any back up sources?

(8) Is this a product or service that needs to researched, developed, improved, designed or redesigned? If yes,

    (a)   Who will do it?

    (b)   Where?

    (c)   How much will it cost?

    (d)   How long will it take?

    (e)   Is it protectable by patent or other means?

(9) How will you maintain quality control?

(10) Do you have a means of staying current with technology and market trends?

As mentioned above, stay as objective as possible. When you get too attached to your product or service, you will lose your competitive edge and become careless, unresponsive to changing market conditions and your product will become obsolete.

And don't get caught up in a wonderful idea that can't be profitable.

F.   LEGAL ISSUES

Many businesses are severely impacted by legal issues which, inevitably, translate to money. In some cases, legal issues affect the growth potential of the business; and in others, it is the very existence of the business that is in jeopardy.

a.   Legality

This is one of the issues that affects the existence of the business. Naturally, you wouldn't start a business that you know is illegal. But what are the chances that your business will become illegal either because a law is passed that prohibits it or a local ordinance says you can't operate your business in a particular place?

If you think this is far-fetched, consider the following example:

You open a fast food restaurant next to a high school. Great idea, right? Then the city council passes a zoning ordinance that bans restaurants within 500 yards of the high school because too many students are drawn off campus during school hours and a traffic problem is created. Not such a great idea now.

Now that the issue is one for the lawyers, who are the only ones to come out ahead, does this mean you close the restaurant? Not necessarily. You fight the ordinance, be sensitive to the issues and talk to people. This may seem like a pure legal issue but it's also a political issue – and politics means people. Maybe you can overcome the objections and satisfy the concerns; or maybe you win outright on constitutional grounds.

In short, a little common sense and forethought could prevent the loss of your business.

b.   Warranties

A warranty is the seller's and/or manufacturer's promise to the user that the product and/or service will do what it is supposed to.

If you have poor quality control and you're selling defective merchandise which is returned and exchanged for new items, your costs will go way up and you'll lose money.

Also, if your warranty is too long, you are exposing yourself to liability for that period. For example, if you give a 3-year warranty covering a particular problem and sell a product today, you won't know for 3 years what your actual cost on that sale is. We can deal with it by estimating what percentage of sales is allocated to warranty expense; but the fact is that the product you sell today could be back in 2 years and 11 months.

The joke that products seem to break down right after the warranty expires is not based on coincidence. Extensive research and testing tells a manufacturer (at least one that can afford the testing) when the product will start to have problems based on some "average" use. By terminating the warranty prior to that problem date, the manufacturer can save itself a tremendous amount of expense.

On the other hand, as mentioned earlier, warranties are also a marketing tool. So don't get caught with too limited a warranty, otherwise your competition might use it as a weapon against you.

c.   Liability

The liability issues discussed below are not the kind of liabilities that come up in the normal course of business, such as contractual and warranty. The following are liabilities that arise when something has gone wrong.

(1) Personal Injury

People can come into your store or office and get hurt by falling or from some other cause. This can be covered by insurance, but your planning concern is what the likelihood of someone getting hurt is and what the cost to insure against such likelihood is.

In an office, for instance, the chance of someone getting hurt is one thing. In a workshop or automotive garage the chance is much greater. There are signs at garages that customers are not allowed in the work area so the insurance rates will not have to cover the chance of an untrained customer wandering around.

PROPER PLANNING CAN KEEP INSURANCE PREMIUMS TO A MINIMUM. Many insurance agencies will assist you in keeping your costs down by suggesting means of accident prevention.

(2) Property

Things (not just people) can get damaged, which can be covered by insurance. Unlike damages for personal injury which can include "pain and suffering" and future wages, damages for property loss are generally limited to replacement cost, which is a much more predictable figure. Consequently, you can weigh the premiums against the cost and what steps you can take to minimize premiums.

SOMETIMES BUSINESSES 'SELF INSURE' AGAINST PROPERTY DAMAGE, meaning they accept the risk of loss which can be estimated fairly closely. Self-insurance is, itself, a risk and should not be undertaken lightly. Those who view self-insurance as a way of not paying for insurance are risking a great deal.

(3) Product Liability

You might sell a product that is defective, either in its design or the manufacture of that specific item, and that product causes injury in its normal use. This is similar to personal injury, except it can happen anywhere. At your place of business if, for instance, you have a restaurant and are serving food that makes people sick or at the buyer's home if, for instance, you sell a toaster that starts a fire causing injury.

Even if you're retailer who bought the item from a wholesaler who bought it from the manufacturer, you're still liable. You can go after the wholesaler and manufacturer to get them to cover you, but the purchaser can go after anyone in the distribution chain.

Product liability insurance is, for many manufacturers, a very costly expense because it is such an unknown. Product liability insurance can also be used as a marketing tool, however, where one manufacturer uses the fact that it has such insurance while competitors do not. The difference to a purchaser is that the purchaser knows the manufacturer has the financial ability to stand behind its product whereas the manufacturer without insurance might go broke if the damage is too great.

d.   Form or organization

This is a topic that comes up again in the financing and legal sections. It's relevant here because:

It's the skeleton on which the business exists, and it's a major consideration to investors who want to know that they are insulated from certain liability problems.

The specifics of the alternatives are discussed in other sections of this book, so for now we'll simply list the choices and major features:

(1) Sole proprietorship

    (a)   No other investors

    (b)   Unlimited liability of the owner

    (c)   Direct taxation of profits and losses

(2) General partnership

    (a)   Unlimited liability of the partners

    (b)   Equal control over the business unless partners agree otherwise

    (c)   Direct taxation of profits and losses

(3) Limited partnership

    (a) Unlimited liability of general partner; limited liability of limited partners

    (b) Management exclusively by the general partner

    (c) Direct taxation of profits and losses

(4) Corporation

    (a) Limited liability of shareholders

    (b) Management by officers

    (c) Double taxation of distributed profits

(5) Sub-Chapter S Corporation

    (a) Same as Corporation except direct taxation of profits and losses

    (b) Applies for federal purposes but not in all states.

G. MANAGEMENT

You must know what capabilities you'll need, as well as the strengths and weaknesses of people already available to you. Those will help you determine what gaps exist.

You must then convince financiers that you have the personnel and capabilities to execute. While you might rely on your "gut," financiers won't - they want track record. Since track record is often difficult for a new business to obtain, it just means you'll have tougher time getting investment capital. It doesn't mean you shouldn't move forward, though.

You should ask yourself and answer in the plan the following questions, being specific about names, job descriptions and experience:

a. Who's responsible for what?

    (1) General management

    (2) Strategic planning

    (3) Marketing and sales

    (4) Manufacturing

    (5) Accounting and finance

b.   What independent consultants are you working with?

    (1) Lawyer

    (2) Accountant

    (3) Public relations

    (4) Advertising

    (5) Etc.

c.   How is management compensated?

d.   What ownership does management have in the company and how much is management investing (if anything)?

e.   What consideration has been given to future management and training?

H. RISK

This section is probably the most controversial in the entire plan. You're supposed to state all the problems and everything that can go wrong. This section doesn't convey information so much as it serves as a shield for the entrepreneur. Unfortunately, this section is also contrary to what you're trying to do in the plan - namely, sell an idea.

The following are kinds of statements you might see in the Risk section (while my comments in parentheses are not).

> "The business has no operating history." *(Since you're starting a new business, this seems fairly obvious.)*

"There is intense competition." *(Very often you say this even if you're the only game in town.)*

"There is no guarantee the business will be able to achieve the sales projected." *(Anyone who can guarantee projections should live in Las Vegas!)*

"There is no guarantee the business will be able to obtain the product or service at current prices." *(Unless you have a long term contract, how many people assume prices will never change?)*

"Management has limited experience in this business." *(The experience of management should be described in detail in the Management section; and if the reader didn't understand the detail, it is questionable he/she will even get to this part. But it's here anyway.)*

I. FINANCE

Here we are at the bottom line. How much does it cost and how much can we make. Could we say it any simpler? The difficulty many people run into is that they believe it is that simple.

Example:

You have an idea to manufacture and sell widgets for $10.00. In fact, you already have an order for 10,000 widgets at $100,000. You can buy the parts for $2.00, so you tell people your profit is $80,000 on that sale alone.

How much will it cost to:

- Assemble the parts?
- Package the goods?
- Ship the goods?
- Get insurance?

- Pay for office rent and expenses?
- Pay payroll and payroll taxes?
- Cover warranty expense?
- etc., etc., etc.

If you're not scared off yet, let's move ahead and try to figure out where our money's coming from.

DON'T FORGET: THE BUSINESS PLAN IS WRITTEN FOR DIFFERENT GROUPS OF PEOPLE AND INSTITUTIONS. You may be presenting your plan to a lender and an investor at the same time, each of whom has deal structures he/she/it is comfortable with. You will want to tailor your proposed deal structure for the particular party you're making the presentation to. For example, don't present an equity investment to a savings & loan which only lends money; and don't go to a venture capital company and expect to get loan rates competitive to that of a bank.

a.   Capitalization

This is the "how much" section in which you tell people:

(1) What form of organization you'll use? This issue is critical to an investor who wants to be protected from liability for debts of the business or lawsuits.

(2) How much the business will need?

(3) What the "deal" is for someone who puts in capital. Since the projection focuses on what dollar amount an investor might get back, this paragraph deals with the terms of the deal, including percentages, duration of the investment and other considerations:

   (a) How many shares? What percentage of the total does this represent?

   (b) What interest rates do lenders or preferred shareholders receive and for how long?

b.   Use of Proceeds

This section describes how you expect to spend the money, whether it's yours, lenders', investors' or a combination.

You should do this in 2 formats:

- In summary form where you list major items of expense (rent, salary, inventory, advertising, etc.)

- In monthly form where you show the major items and the timing of the expenses indicated in the summary.

c.   Projections

What do you expect the business to accomplish financially? This is where you present:

(1) Your projections of income (usually for 24-48 months). Projections are guesses, at best; but some people will still say you "promised" certain results. Don't make it any worse by stating projections as facts. Just be reasonable; and don't be too optimistic or pessimistic.

(2) Cash flow projections for the same period as the income forecast. The difference between this and the income projection is that you take into account the fact that you don't necessarily pay a bill the day you incur it and you don't receive cash the day you make the sale. The failure to recognize this difference can be one of the biggest mistakes any businessperson can make.

(3) Your balance sheet - usually at the end of each 12 month period included in your income projections.

d.   Returns

What do the owners and lenders (including investors, if any) get in return for their commitment to the business?

What is the dollar amount return projected for each of the owners/investors and lenders, and over what period of time?

e.   Timetable

One item that few business plans have but is very helpful to you as an entrepreneur, and to people trying to understand your business, is an overall timetable. Such a timetable encompasses all aspects of the business, not just financial.

I've included this in the Finance section because this is where most people look to see what you believe will be happening to the business.

IV. FORMS OF ORGANIZATION

A. SOLE PROPRIETORSHIP

a. Definition: A sole proprietorship is a business owned by one person. From a practical point of view, the owner may keep the business and his/her personal life separate; but from a legal perspective, there is no distinction between the individual's personal life and his/her business. There are no other owners of the business.

b. Liability: Since there is no legal distinction between a sole proprietor's business and his/her personal life, a sole proprietor has unlimited liability for all debts of the business. If you start a business as a sole proprietor, the business incurs debts and you later discontinue the business without paying those debts, your business creditors can come after you personally.

c. Life: The life of a sole proprietorship is limited to the life of the sole proprietor.

d. Taxability: Since there is no legal distinction between the personal and business life of a sole proprietor, the sole proprietor gets taxed on everything the business activity makes. This *flow-through* aspect of taxation is beneficial if (1) the sole proprietor is taking all the profits out of the business, or (2) the business is losing money and the sole proprietor has other income (including a spouse's) against which to take deductions, thereby reducing total taxable income. In the US, the income or loss of a sole proprietorship is reported on Schedule C of your federal income tax forms.

e. Ease of formation: Forming a sole proprietorship is very easy. In most states, all that you need to do is file a *Fictitious Business Name Statement* (aka *dba*) or the equivalent, publish it as required by your local jurisdiction and get a business license from your city.

f. Transferability of Interests: Since there is no distinction between a sole proprietor and his/her business, you can't transfer a sole proprietorship. You can sell the assets (furniture, inventory and even goodwill); but you can't sell *the company*.

g.   Ability to Raise Capital: The ability to raise capital is limited in two respects:

   (1) If you raise equity (money that does not have to be repaid) from one or more persons and have additional owners, then you aren't a *sole proprietorship* anymore.

   (2) Your liability to obtain debt is limited by whatever criteria a bank would look at in making you a personal loan.

h.   Management Rights: Since you are the only owner, you have all the management rights and can delegate the responsibilities anyway you choose. Keep in mind, though, the liability of a principal for acts of his/her agents or employees and the fact that a sole proprietor has unlimited liability.

B.   GENERAL PARTNERSHIP

a.   Definition: People often use a word or phrase to convey a concept rather than a specific statement. For instance, "partnership" is commonly used to describe any relationship between people who are owners of a business. In fact, being "partners" has some very special legal characteristics.

   A general partnership is the business conducted by two or more individuals each of whom is a *general partner*. This is the entity and relationship we usually refer to as *partnership* and *partners*. Like a sole proprietorship, there is no distinction between the individual partners' personal lives and their business.

b.   Capital vs. Income: In any business, there are 2 ways to make money. The first is by appreciation of the assets and the second is by income. The latter is obvious, and an example of the former is where you buy a piece of property and over time it simply gets more valuable.

   In a general partnership, these 2 avenues are evidenced by interest in the capital of the business (the business itself) and interest in the profits and losses. General partners can allocate the interests in capital and profits any way they please; provided they do so by agreement. Most states have a "Uniform Partnership Act" which specifies certain aspects of the partnership unless otherwise by the parties. It is called "Uniform" by the states that have adopted it in an effort to make the laws from state to state consistent. This makes interpretation and enforcement of the law easier and discourages formation of partnerships in a particular state solely because of the rules that apply. This last element is something that is a major consideration in the formation of corporations and the reason that so many corporations are incorporated in states such as Delaware, New Jersey and Maryland.

As a partner, you can create a partnership with whatever terms you want; but if you don't specify the terms, the Uniform Partnership Act will do it for you. For instance, if the partners do not have a specific agreement as to how profits and losses are divided, the UPA gives all the partners equal interest – *regardless who put what money in*. If the partners have agreed on one of these items, the other is presumed to be allocated in the same proportion.

Assume in the following examples that there is no agreement between the partners as to how capital, profits and losses will be distributed, except where stated.

> (1) Bill and Joe each invest $1000 in a business that they will run together. They have no agreement as to the division of capital, profits or losses, so the UPA says they'll share everything 50-50.

> (2) Bill puts up $2000, and Joe will do all the work. The UPA says they share everything 50-50.

> (3) Sherry puts up an additional $1000 to the $2000 put up by Bill in the previous example, but Sherry does no work. When Sherry comes in, the partners agree that Sherry will get 20% of the company even though she put up 33% of the money and Sherry will get 100% of the profits and losses until she gets her money back and then they will all share equally.

Hopefully, you see the importance of having a partnership agreement which, among other things, allocates capital and income. If, for some reason, you do not have an agreement, the UPA will settle the issue; although not always the way you anticipated when you got into the partnership.

c. Liability: Since there is no distinction between each partner's business and his/her personal life, all general partners have unlimited liability for all debts of the business. This means that if you start a business as a general partner, the business then incurs debts and you later discontinue the business without having paid those debts, your business creditors can come after you personally. This is true even if the creditors could have gone after your partner(s).

The partners' liability is *joint and several*, meaning that each partner can be held liable for <u>all</u> partnership liabilities. The partner being held liable can go after the other partners to come up with their shares; but it's the partner's obligation to go after the other partners not the creditor's.

Example: You have an electronics shop. Your partner is at an electronics show where he sees the biggest new TV and signs a purchase order for 3 at $5000 each. When your partner gets back, he tells you what he did and you know you'll never sell those TV's. The manufacturer refuses to cancel the order. You could be personally liable for this order that was created by your agent (partner).

The practical effect of this is that a wealthy individual will almost never get into a general partnership with someone who doesn't have as much or more assets since, if there's a liability the partnership can't pay, the creditor is going right for the wealthy partner without even looking at the other partners. This also puts the partners in a position of conflict if they had not already agreed that the wealthy partner would pay all additional debts of the business.

d. Life: A general partnership is a concept heavily rooted in the personal relationship between the partners. The basic position of the law is that you should not be forced to be the partner of someone you do not choose. Consequently, each partner owes the other partners a fiduciary duty which, as discussed in the Agency section, is the highest possible duty of loyalty and trust.

Consequently, the life of a general partnership is limited to the life of any general partner. A specific agreement can, however, provide for continuation of the business by the remaining partners. This is another reason for having a partnership agreement.

e. Taxability: The flow-through taxation of a sole proprietorship applies to a general partnership as if there were no distinction between the personal and business life of each partner. The benefits of flow-through taxation are the same here as in sole proprietorships. A partnership files a partnership tax return, though it pays no taxes. Each partner includes the profits or losses on his /her personal income tax returns and, for US federal income tax purposes, files a K-1 form prepared by the partnership.

f. Ease of formation: Forming a general partnership is very easy. In most states, all you need do is file a "Fictitious Business Name Statement" or the equivalent, publish it as required by your local jurisdiction and get a business license from the city. Such ease can, as pointed out, create some very messy problems. If the rules established by the Uniform Partnership Act are not what you intended to govern your relationship, it's best to spend a little more time (and maybe money) to create a partnership agreement that spells out the way you want the relationship to be.

g. Management Rights: Regardless how capital, profits and losses are divided, the Uniform Partnership Act gives each partner an equal right to possession of the assets and management of the business. Any limitations placed upon the management rights of the partners must be done by agreement between the parties.

h. Transferability of Interests: Each partner owns an undivided interest in the partnership. This means that if, for instance, a partnership of 3 people owned 3 cars of equal value, each partner would own 1/3 of all 3 cars; as opposed to each partner owning 1 car.

A partnership interest is generally not transferable based on the principle stated earlier that you shouldn't be forced to be partners with someone not of your choosing. However, a partner who wants to sell or give away his/her interest can give away his rights to share in the capital and profit of the business, but not his right to share in the management of the business or possession of the assets, unless approved by the other partners.

i. Ability to Raise Capital

(a)　Equity: Unlike a sole proprietorship, a partnership can raise equity capital by selling general partnership interests. As mentioned above, selling a general partnership interest to a passive investor (someone who is relying on you to do all the work) is a difficult approach.

(b)　Debt: Your ability to raise debt is still generally limited by the personal creditworthiness of the partners. Remembering that liability is joint and several, a lender need only feel comfortable that at least one of the partners will be able to pay the debt in case of default by the partnership.

C.　LIMITED PARTNERSHIP

a.　Definition: A limited partnership is the business conducted by two or more individuals where at least one person is a general partner and one or more partners are *limited*.

As in the case of partnerships, most states have a law governing the relationships in a limited partnership. The law is called "The Uniform Limited Partnership Act."

Unlike a general partnership, however, there <u>must</u> be a written agreement to form a limited partnership. Absent such an agreement and qualifying procedures, the partners are general, which may be totally contrary to the intentions of the parties...especially those who expected to be *limited* partners.

This vehicle is a commonly chosen form of organization for a new business that requires more capital than the entrepreneur can come up with his own resources or that of immediate family and friends as loans.

b.   Liability: The general partner of a limited partnership has the same liability as a general partner in a general partnership - unlimited. Provided the qualifying procedures set out by each state are satisfied, the limited partners' liability is limited to what they agreed to in the Limited Partnership Agreement. Generally, this is their initial capital contribution. A limited partner would not be liable for the TV's in the example mentioned above.

Unlike a general partnership, limited partners cannot bind the partnership to anything. So, while the general partner has unlimited liability, it will only be from acts done or incurred by him or herself. Of course, if there is more than one general partner, the same situations arise with respect to the agency relationship between the general partners of a limited partnership as existed in the general partnership.

Like a general partnership, a limited partnership is based on the personal relationships between the partners. The fiduciary duty mentioned earlier, therefore, applies to the general partner's obligation to the limited partners.

c.   Life: The same rules apply as in the case of a general partnership. The difference is that provision is almost always made for continuation of the business following the death or disability of a partner; even the general partner.

d.   Taxability: The principle of flow-through taxation applies. Since profits and losses can be allocated any way the partners choose (provided the allocation is not principally for tax avoidance), a common feature of limited partnership agreements is that the partners putting up the money (the limited partners) get all the losses (therefore, all the deductions and tax benefits, if any) and all the profits until they make their initial investment back. Only then does the general partner share in profits and losses of the business.

In the US, the limited partnership files a Limited Partnership Tax Return even though it does not pay taxes. Each partner gets a K1 statement from the partnership showing his/her or its portion of the profits or losses from the partnership, which are then included in the partner's individual tax return.

e.   Ease of information: Forming a limited partnership can be more expensive than a general partnership because it requires an agreement and certain filings; and because many of the investors will have the business plan and limited partnership agreement reviewed by their attorneys and/or accountants. If you're starting a business using the Limited Partnership form of organization and you want to credibility with your prospective partners, it is best you have the agreement drafted by an attorney. In addition to the Limited Partnership Agreement, you will likely need some other forms and documents; and this is where you need to remember to ask a professional.

f.   Transferability of Interests: Each partner owns an *undivided* interest in the partnership. Due to all the restrictions imposed by the limited partnership agreement and created by state and federal laws, such investments are relatively *illiquid* (meaning difficult to sell).

Limited partnership Agreements generally provide for certain rights of first refusal which give the limited partnership, its general partner(s) and/or remaining limited partner(s) the right to purchase the interest before the selling partner can offer the interest to anyone else. This makes the process of selling a partnership interest more cumbersome and time consuming.

The person buying the interest already has limited management rights but purchasing an interest outside of the approved channels as determined by the limited partnership agreement might even limit such purchasing partner's rights to just examining the books of the partnership.

g.   Ability to Raise Capital

(a)   Equity: Limited partnerships are familiar to many investors, attorneys and accountants. Assuming you can convince a prospective investor that your idea is a good investment, the objections that need to be overcome by the promoter are the ones discussed here, the most significant being limited transferability.

(b)   Debt: If you are the only general partner and your limited partners have no obligation for debts of the business, your ability to raise debt is the same as if you were a sole proprietor. However, the limited partnership form of organization seems to most people to be a more substantial and stable form of business which will, by virtue of the investment by yourself and the limited partners, have assets that may be used as collateral for new loans.

h.   Management Rights: The right of limited partners to participate in management of the business is limited to events that would change the nature of the business or their investment. Day-to-day involvement is prohibited and such participation could jeopardize their standing as a limited partner, which, if lost, could result in their being held liable as a general partner for company obligations and liabilities, which is something wealthy individuals expressly wanted to avoid by choosing to be a *limited partner*.

D.   CORPORATION

a.   Definition: A corporation is a legal entity separate from its owners, regardless how many. Each state grants a *charter* for a corporation which gives it the status of a legal "person" with the same rights to own property, sue and be sued as a person.

All states have extensive sets of laws governing the operation of corporations, including the mandatory procedures for creating a corporation.

While limited partnerships are a common form of raising capital for a venture, corporations are, outside of persons rendering personal services (such as doctors, plumbers, etc.) the most common form of doing business in America.

b.   Liability: One of the reasons corporations are a popular form of doing business is that the corporation can protect its owners and employees from liability for debts and obligations of the business.

Consequently, if a customer in your TV shop slips and injures himself and sues the business and its shareholders, the shareholders should – if the corporation was formed properly and is being run properly – be shielded from liability.

There are, however, some circumstances under which the shareholders would still be liable notwithstanding the corporation. When an attorney is trying to reach the shareholders, it is called *piercing the corporate veil*. Some examples of when the corporate veil might be pierced and the shareholders held liable for obligations of the business are:

> The shareholders comingle business and personal funds (failing to properly distinguish personal and business assets and activities). This includes paying business bills from personal accounts and not properly accounting for these transactions.

> The shareholders did not adequately capitalize the business for what might reasonably be anticipated.

> The shareholders otherwise conduct the business in a way that blurs the distinction between the corporate organization and themselves as shareholders.

c. Transferability of Interests: Shares in a corporation are, theoretically, freely transferable. The reality is that (1) you cannot advertise the availability of your stock unless the corporation has *registered* the stock under various federal and state securities laws, and (2) in a small corporation all the stock of which is owned by a few people (the corporation is then considered "closely held"), the shareholders will generally have a Shareholders Agreement which limits their right to transfer stock and creates a right of first refusal, similar to that of the limited partnership agreement. Consequently, the transferability of stock of closely held corporations is still very difficult because there are not a lot of people out there rushing to buy such restricted stock.

d.	Ability to Raise Capital: Corporations are, by far, the most common vehicle for raising money from investors because of the limited liability and free transferability features.

Though the corporation protects the individual from liability on corporate obligations, the reality is that in order to obtain certain loans, one or more of the owners (shareholders) may have to give up that protection by guaranteeing the corporation's obligations under the terms of that loan.

e.	Management Rights: At the start, the shareholders, directors and employees might all be the same people. However, the shareholders of a corporation, even though they're the owners, have no right to participate in the day-to-day management of the business. The shareholders' rights are to elect a Board of Directors which, in turn, selects a management team. As the company gets bigger and, possibly, has many shareholders, the practice of consulting all the shareholders in day-to-day management affairs will quickly become a problem.

f.	Sub-Chapter S Corporation: In the U.S., everything about a *Sub-Chapter S Corporation* is the same as for a regular Corporation, as described above, except taxation.

Sometimes the form of organization that makes the most business sense, apart from taxation, is a corporation. The tax treatment, however, may be a disincentive to create that business. Since our system of free enterprise depends on new business and entrepreneurs, the Sub-Chapter S election for corporations was created.

This is an election that can be made by a corporation to take advantage of the flow-through characteristics described above for partnerships. This can be very advantageous when:

(1)	The business is in a startup phase and losing money. With this election the shareholders can deduct the losses from their other income.

(2)   All the profits are being distributed to the shareholders, thereby avoiding double taxation.

Note that if you make a Sub-Chapter S election you can terminate it later. Also, the Sub-Chapter S election is provided in the US by the Internal Revenue Service for federal tax purposes. Some states do not provide such an election, meaning that for state tax purposes the flow-through taxation does not apply and dividends (distributed profits) will be subject to double taxation while losses cannot be deducted against the personal income of the owners.

E.   LIMITED LIABILITY COMPANY

a. Definition: A limited liability company ("LLC") is a hybrid of a corporation and limited partnership. It is easily formed and has characteristics of each.

The owners are called *members*. The member who is operating the business (as opposed to the passive investors) is called the *managing member*. Unlike a limited partnership in which the general partner has unlimited liability, the managing member of an LLC, like the other members, has limited liability based on the same circumstances described above for corporations relative to *piercing the corporate veil*.

Like the limited partnership, income and losses are taxed on the flow-through basis and can be allocated in as the members may determine.

Whereas a corporation may have By-laws and a Shareholders Agreement among the owners and partners in a limited partnership have a Limited Partnership Agreement, members of an LLC have an *Operating Agreement* which sets out the rights and the relationships of the members and how the organization will function.

V.   ACCOUNTING

There are 3 objectives to this Chapter:

1. Understanding a little about basic accounting.

2. Understanding the formats generally used to convey information about financial position and performance.

3. Gaining an awareness of some of the issues, questions and choices that businesses encounter.

A.   BASIC ACCOUNTING

As in much of this book, the goal is not to give you a lot of information to memorize. The goal is to give you enough information so that if the subject comes up, you'll remember there's a question to be asked.

You may wonder why you should know about accounting. There are many accounting programs such as QuickBooks that make the task of *bookkeeping* easy. But as anyone who has ever watched the popular TV shows "Shark Tank" or "Dragon's Den" knows, investors expect entrepreneurs to be very familiar with their own finances; and accounting is the means by which you obtain the information to make decisions as well as analyze performance. In addition, understanding the building blocks of our accounting system will help you better understand the financial statements you will use and how other people will view your business.

Accounting is not simply a record of what happened. There are accounting choices which can have significant effects on your business. For instance, if you want to build your assets you might buy a building; but if you want to reduce your taxable income you might rent. Choices you make with regard to inventory and equipment can make big differences - without doing anything differently. Despite financial limitations, you still should know what options you have.

Another reason for knowing something about basic accounting is control. After all, how do you feel when you go to the doctor or auto mechanic who tells you something's wrong and that to fix it will cost $x? Do you know if he/she is right? I don't. But if you have a little knowledge, you can ask enough of the right questions to feel a little more comfortable - knowing you can't be blindly led into financial ruin.

1.   Accountant vs Bookkeeper

The 2 biggest differences between a bookkeeper and an accountant are:

> 1. The bookkeeper records the transactions in the books whereas the accountant also makes some strategic decisions, and

> 2. The accountant has more training and gets paid more.

Most people and small businesses have fairly simple books which could be handled by themselves using a computer program or by a bookkeeper. The "books" that a bookkeeper maintains are the "Journal" and the "Ledger" (each is described below). However, sometimes outsiders who need to see your "books and records" or financial statements may want a Certified Public Accountant to be involved.

A Certified Public Accountant is an accountant who has had specified training and has passed an examination given throughout the United States. It is not an easy examination and, in fact, only about 5% of the people who take the exam pass it the first time.

In selecting a bookkeeper, accountant or CPA, it's nice to have someone who's had some experience with your type of business. More importantly, however, is getting someone you trust and who is strong enough to admit he or she doesn't know something. On the other hand, you don't want someone who's trustworthy but doesn't know anything.

Ask people you trust for recommendations. Talk to several bookkeepers and/or accountants and compare. A bad bookkeeper or accountant can hurt you a lot.

2.   The Journal

The journal is where you (or the computer software you're using) record the transactions you make. Everything goes in here. If you buy or sell something, if something gets old, or if you make money or pay a bill, it's all here.

Sometimes the bookkeeper will come in once a week or you'll do the books yourself every so often. You should still record the transactions as of the day each occurred. That way, you can see all the activity on a given day or in a given period without searching through every entry to match the day or period. The Journal is like sorting your email by date.

3.   Ledger

The ledger is the companion book to the journal. In the journal you see things as they occurred. In the Ledger you see all activity of a particular kind. For instance, you pay your phone bill once a month. At the end of the year, if you wanted to find out what your total phone bills were, you could go through the journal and add up the phone payments whenever you found one or you could look in the ledger at the "phone account." It would show you all the activity of the phone bills throughout the year. The ledger is like sorting your email by subject or by sender.

4.   The Double Entry System

Before we can see how the journal and ledger fit together, we need one more piece to the puzzle - the key to our entire accounting system: the double entry.

Imagine a balancing scale with the left side called "debit" and the right side called "credit." The system works because the scale is always balanced. To be that way, debits always have to equal credits. There are no exceptions. This is the reason a "Balance Sheet" is called a "Balance Sheet."

The following is a list of what kinds of things are debits and credits. You don't have to memorize them ... just try to understand the concepts and you will be able to figure it out when you have to.

If you INCREASE an ASSET it's a DEBIT

If you DECREASE an ASSET it's a CREDIT

Assets include:

- Cash
- Accounts Receivable (when people owe us money)
- Inventory
- Buildings
- Land
- Equipment

If you INCREASE a LIABILITY it's a CREDIT

If you DECREASE a LIABILITY it's a DEBIT

Liabilities include:

- Accounts & Notes Payable (when you owe others money)
- Deposits (when you're holding someone else's money even if it might be yours at some point)

If you INCREASE EQUITY it's a CREDIT

If you DECREASE EQUITY it's a DEBIT

Equity is the money you invest in the business and make in profit (or lose). It's what's yours after all the debts are paid.

Equity includes:

- Capital Stock (the investment)
- Retained Earnings (the amount you've made and not given to the shareholders, or lost).

If you INCREASE INCOME it's a CREDIT

If you DECREASE INCOME it's a DEBIT

Income is money you earn for goods and services.

If you INCREASE EXPENSES it's a DEBIT

If you DECREASE EXPENSES it's a CREDIT

Expenses are the costs of running a business.

Another way to remember this is:

DEBITS:

- Increase Assets
- Increase Expense
- Decrease Liabilities
- Decrease Equity

CREDITS:

- Decrease Income
- Decrease Assets
- Decrease Expenses
- Increase Liabilities
- Increase Equity
- Increase Income

For example, say you fixed someone's garage door and he paid you $100 cash. The journal entry for that transaction would be:

Date	Description	Account	Debit	Credit
1/1	Cash		$100	
	Income			$100

You then pay for some supplies you used fixing the garage

Date	Description	Account	Debit	Credit
1/2	Supply Expense		$100	
	Cash			$100

Each transaction has 2 parts - a debit and a credit. "Cash" appears as a debit in the first entry and as a credit in the second. This is because in the first case you increased your cash and in the second you reduced your cash.

5.   Using the Books

Now you're ready to put the puzzle together with a series of transactions.

1. On Jan. 1 you put $5,000 into your TV repair business.

The journal entry is:

Date	Description	Account	Debit	Credit
1/1	Cash		$5,000	
	Capital Stock			$5,000

You debit Cash because you increased the cash in the business; and credit Capital Stock (in the Equity part of the Balance Sheet) because you increased Equity. [The "Credit" entry is indented a little to make it easier to identify.] The date helps you find everything that happened on a particular date. The "Account number" refers to the ledger; meaning that "cash" is account #001 and "Capital" is account #301. At the end of the month, you'll transfer (or your computer software will do it automatically) the journal entries to the respective ledger account, each of which is kept on a separate page for easy reference (if you're doing it by hand).

For this example, the ledger accounts would look like:

CASH #001

Date	Description	Debit	Credit
1/1	Capital contribution	$5,000	

CAPITAL STOCK #301

Date	Description	Debit	Credit
1/1	You		$5,000

The debit entry in the journal is still a debit in the ledger, and the same is true for the credit entry.

2. On Jan. 1 you pay $500 first month's rent for your office.

The journal entry is:

Date	Description	Account	Debit	Credit
1/1	January rent expense	501	$5,000	
	Cash	001		$5,000

You increased an expense of running the business, which is a debit. You also decreased an asset (cash), so it's a credit.

The ledger accounts would be:

RENT EXPENSE #501

Date	Description	Debit	Credit
1/1	January rent		$500

CASH #001

Date	Description		Debit	Credit
1/1	Capital contribution		$5,000	
1/1	January rent			$500
		Balance	$4500	

You created a new account, "Rent Expense" and you had another cash transaction. This time you reduced cash, which is a credit. Your new cash balance is $4500 ($5000-$500), which is much easier to see by looking at the Cash account in the ledger than by going through all the journal entries.

3. On Jan. 3 you buy $1000 of equipment to use in your business on 30 day credit.

The journal entry is:

Date	Description	Account	Debit	Credit
1/1	Equipment	003	$1,000	
	Capital Stock	101		$1,000

You increased an asset account (Equipment), so it's a debit; and you increased a liability account (Accounts Payable are amounts you owe to normal, everyday suppliers), so it's a credit.

The ledger accounts look like:

EQUIPMENT #003

Date	Description	Debit	Credit
1/3	Equipment	$1,000	

ACCOUNTS PAYABLE #101

Date	Description	Debit	Credit
1/3	Equipment purchase		$1,000

4. On Jan. 5 you fix a TV and get paid $50.

The journal entry is:

Date	Description	Account	Debit	Credit
1/5	Cash	001	$50	
	Income	401		$50

You received cash, so you debit "Cash"; and you generated income so you credit "Income."

The ledger accounts look like:

CASH #001

Date	Description		Debit	Credit
1/1	Capital contribution		$5,000	
1/1	January rent			$500
1/5	Income		$50	
		Balance	$4550	

(The $4550 balance is the difference between the debits and the credits.)

INCOME #401

Date	Description	Debit	Credit
1/5	TV Repair		$50

5. On Jan. 7 you fix a TV for $75 but the customer is going to pay you by the end of the month.

The journal entry is:

Date	Description	Account	Debit	Credit
1/7	Accounts Receivable	002	$75	
	Income	401		$75

You generated income by fixing a TV, so credit "Income." Instead of getting cash, though, you have an "Account Receivable," meaning someone owes you money in the normal everyday course of business. "Accounts Receivable" is an asset account, so debit "Accounts Receivable."

The ledger looks like:

ACCOUNTS RECEIVABLE #002

Date	Description	Debit	Credit
1/1	TV Repair	$75	

INCOME # 401

Date	Description	Debit	Credit
1/5	TV Repair		$50
1/7	TV Repair		$75
	Balance		$125

6. On Jan. 10 someone brings you a TV to fix. You tell the customer it needs some parts which will take 30 days to get, and the customer says okay.

There is no journal entry since the TV isn't yours and you haven't rendered a service yet. In fact, nothing's happened except that you're keeping someone's TV in your shop until the parts come in.

When one person takes care of someone else's property, the legal term for this is "bailment." The person who owns the property is called the "bailer" and the person who is taking care of the property is the "bailee." A coat check room where there's an attendant is also a bailment, as is a valet parking lot. Different kinds of bailments create different legal obligations.

7. On Jan. 15 you hire a helper at $10.00 an hour to work 40 hours per week.

There's no journal entry because the worker is just starting and you don't owe him any money yet. When, for instance, a major league baseball team acquires a player in a trade, though, they treat that person - or rather his contract - as an asset. The amounts to be paid under that contract are liabilities.

8. On Jan. 17 you receive a TV to fix and, because it's a pretty big job, you ask for a deposit of $100.

The journal entry is:

Date	Description	Account	Debit	Credit
1/17	Cash	001	$100	
	Deposits	102		$100

What's different about this than #6? In this case, you've actually gotten something - a deposit. You increase your cash account by debiting "Cash."

What's "Customer Deposit" and why are you crediting it?

A "customer deposit" is, theoretically, money that still belongs to the customer which you might have to give back: so it's a liability. When you increase a liability, it's a credit. This is why when you make a deposit into your bank account the bank "credits" your account. The bank is increasing its liabilities: the amount of other people's money the bank is holding and has to give back at some point. On the bank's books, it's a CREDIT. When you take money out of the bank, they debit your account; meaning they are reducing the amount of money they owe you (because it was yours anyway).

The ledger looks like:

CASH #001

Date	Description		Debit	Credit
1/1	Capital contribution		$5,000	
1/1	January rent			$500
1/5	Income		$50	
1/17	Customer deposit		$100	
		Balance	$4650	

CUSTOMER DEPOSIT #102

Date	Description	Debit	Credit
1/17	TV repair		$100

9. On Jan. 19 a TV manufacturer comes to you and says he has too many and he'd like to sell one to you for you to resell in your store. You pay $100 for the TV and put a price of $200 on it.

The journal entry is:

Date	Description	Account	Debit	Credit
1/19	Inventory	003	$100	
	Cash	001		$100

Inventory includes the things you resell to other people. Sometimes people give you their property to resell for them and they say, "Keep 15% of whatever you get for it." When you're selling property that belongs to someone else, you're holding his or her property on "consignment." The owner is the "consignor" and the person who has possession of the item is the "consignee." The difference between a bailment and consignment is that a bailee isn't supposed to sell the property.

The ledger looks like:

INVENTORY #003

Date	Description	Debit	Credit
1/19	Purchase inventory	$100	

CASH #001

Date	Description		Debit	Credit
1/1	Capital contribution		$5,000	
1/1	January rent			$500
1/5	Income		$50	
1/17	Customer deposit		$100	
1/19	Inventory purchase			$100
		Balance	$4550	

10. On Jan. 21 someone buys the TV for sale for $200 plus $10 sales tax.

The journal entry is:

Date	Description	Account	Debit	Credit
1/21	Cash	001	$210	
	Income	401		$200
	Sales Tax Payable	103		$10

AND

Date	Description	Account	Debit	Credit
1/21	Cost of Goods Sold	502	$100	
	Inventory	003		$100

Several things are going on here:

First, you collected money by selling the TV you bought on January 19. However, of the $210 cash received, only $200 is Income; the other $10 is sales tax which you have to turn over to the state. Since you don't pay sales tax collected immediately, you owe it to the state, which means it's a liability. Notice, though, that the debit ($210) still equals the total credits ($210). If this were not the case, something would be wrong.

Second, by selling the TV you reduced your inventory by the amount you paid for the TV ($100). The corresponding debit when you reduce inventory is "Cost of Goods Sold."

The ledger looks like:

CASH #001

Date	Description		Debit	Credit
1/1	Capital contribution		$5,000	
1/1	January rent			$500
1/5	Income		$50	
1/17	Customer deposit		$100	
1/19	Inventory purchase			$100
1/21	Income		$200	
		Balance	$4750	

INCOME #401

Date	Description		Debit	Credit
1/5	TV Repair			$50
1/7	TV Repair			$75
1/21	TV Sale			$200
		Balance		$325

SALES TAX PAYABLE #103

Date	Description	Debit	Credit
1/21	TV Sale		$10

COST OF GOODS SOLD #502

Date	Description	Debit	Credit
1/21	Sale	$100	

INVENTORY #003

Date	Description		Debit	Credit
1/19	Purchase inventory		$100	
1/21	Sell inventory			$100
		Balance	$0	

11. On Jan. 25 you pay the bill for the equipment you purchased on Jan. 3.

The journal entry is:

Date	Description	Account	Debit	Credit
1/25	Accounts Payable	101	$1,000	
	Cash	001		$1,000

By paying money you reduce your liabilities, which is a debit. Reducing your cash is a credit.

The ledger looks like:

CASH #001

Date	Description		Debit	Credit
1/1	Capital contribution		$5,000	
1/1	January rent			$500
1/5	Income		$50	
1/17	Customer deposit		$100	
1/19	Inventory purchase			$100
1/21	Income		$200	
1/25	Pay account payable			$1,000
		Balance	$3750	

ACCOUNT PAYABLE #101

Date	Description		Debit	Credit
1/3	Equipment purchase			$1,000
1/25	Pay equipment purchased 1/3		$1,000	
		Balance	$0	

12. On Jan. 31 you pay your helper for 80 hours of work (@ $5.00).

The journal entry for this is not so simple because you can't just take the wages times the number of hours worked. Taxes, unemployment insurance and employer's contributions also play a part. However and with that in mind, if you were recording just the wages in this entry, leaving everything else for another entry, the journal entry would be:

Date	Description	Account	Debit	Credit
1/31	Wage Expense 1/15-31	503	$400	
	Cash	001		$400

The ledger looks like:

WAGE EXPENSE #503

Date	Description	Debit	Credit
1/31	Wage expense 1/15-31	$400	

CASH #001

Date	Description	Debit	Credit
1/1	Capital contribution	$5,000	
1/1	January rent		$500
1/5	Income	$50	
1/17	Customer deposit	$100	
1/19	Inventory purchase		$100
1/21	Income	$200	
1/25	Pay account payable		$1,000
1/31	Wage expense 1/15-31		$400
	Balance	$3350	

REMEMBER: If you want to see everything that happened on a given day or in a particular period of time, look in the journal. If you want to see what happened to particular account, look in the ledger.

6.   The Trial Balance

The "Trial Balance" is a listing of every balance of every account you have in the ledger. Since each journal entry had equal debits and credits, and those entries were transferred to the individual ledger accounts, the total debits in the trial balance must equal the total credits. If they don't, there's a mistake.

B.   FINANCIAL STATEMENTS

1.   The Reason for Financial Statements

a.   What are the "financial statements"?

Now that you have books and records, you have accurate (hopefully) records of what business you've been doing and what it costs to operate. Financial statements, which are the summaries of the various accounts in your ledger, are prepared from your books.

The forms that are generally included in the package of financial statements are:

THE BALANCE SHEET shows what you own and owe.

THE INCOME STATEMENT shows what you made or lost.

THE STATEMENT OF CHANGES IN FINANCIAL POSITION shows where your cash came from and where it went. (This can be different than what profit you made or loss you incurred.)

THE STATEMENT OF RETAINED EARNINGS shows how your equity changed from last year to this year.

There is an important caveat (warning): The financial statements listed above, particularly the Income Statement, assume your business is on-going. However, it is possible to have sales and profits but because of the timing of your cash flow and the difficulty of borrowing - you're broke.

THE KEY TO STARTING AND OPERATING A BUSINESS IS <u>NOT</u> <u>PROFITS</u> -- BUT <u>CASH FLOW</u>. "Profits" are NOT the same thing as cash ... and "profits" do you NO good if you don't have the cash to pay your bills!

If you have sales and accounts receivable, figure out when you'll collect those receivables, allow for problems in collection and time your accounts payable so you don't run short. THE WORST FEELING IN THE WORLD IS TO HAVE A GOOD IDEA AND JUST RUN OUT OF TIME.

Some people say, "The books and financial statements are a wasted effort. I've got $5000 more in my bank account than before. That's how I know if I made money." If this is something you'd say, don't expect to grow. Aside from the fact that this statement is just plain wrong, financial statements are for much more than telling you how much cash you have.

b.   Who uses your financial statements?

- YOU AND YOUR MANAGEMENT TEAM use them to evaluate your own performance, the performance of your employees and to make management decisions for the future.

- BANKS AND OTHER LENDERS use them to decide whether to lend you money.

- INVESTORS use them to decide whether to invest in your business.

- CUSTOMERS use them to decide whether you'll be around long enough to deliver the goods or perform the services desired, and whether to give you money up front as a deposit.

- THE IRS AND OTHER TAXING AGENCIES use them to verify the amount of taxes you owe. (Actually, tax forms are different but are based on your books.)

Imagine how difficult it would be to evaluate your performance and credit worthiness if your records were kept differently than everyone else's. You would be at a major disadvantage if you were compared to others who have records and forms of presentation that lenders and investors are used to seeing, especially compared to another business in your industry even if you performed better.

The use of standard formats and means of presentation is, therefore, critical.

2. The Balance Sheet

a.   Assets = Liabilities + Equity

Look at the sample Balance Sheet enclosed in this book. Notice that it is dated "as of December 31." This means that you look at the assets, liabilities and equity of the company at a specific *moment* in time -- the close of business on December 31, for example. The Income Statement, on the other hand, is based on a *period* of time (e.g., January 1 through December 31).

"Total Assets" equal "Total Liabilities & Equity." This is exactly what you expect to see. Notice that assets and liabilities are broken into "Current" and "Fixed" (also called "Long Term"). As discussed below, "current" assets or liabilities are those that can or will be used or gone within 1 year. The reason for this distinction between current and non-current is that when you or someone else is looking at your business, he or she wants to know the value of the assets you have to operate with or can sell quickly to raise money; or, in the case of liabilities, how much you're going to have to spend in the next year.

Your ASSETS are everything you own (and in some cases, for instances long term leases, things you have the right to use or control for a long time): cash, accounts receivable, inventory, property, equipment, some contracts, supplies, etc.

Your LIABILITIES are everything you owe: accounts payable, mortgages, taxes, payroll, etc.

Your EQUITY is what's left: That's what's yours (or yours and the other owners).

The Balance Sheet relationship is similar to owning a home. Take the value less what you owe and that's your equity.

$$VALUE - DEBT = EQUITY$$

Bring up those old memories of algebra and change this around a little by adding "debt" to both sides (sound familiar?) and you get:

$$VALUE = DEBT + EQUITY$$

Or for our purposes,

$$ASSETS = LIABILITIES + EQUITY$$

b.   Historical Cost

A very big difference between the formula for your home and business financial statements is the principal of "historical cost." In the above equation for your home, you plug the current market value into "Value." However, for purposes of a balance sheet, we use the cost of the assets or market value, whichever is LESS. In other words, you don't use market value unless it's less than the cost of the asset. While the purpose of this is to be more conservative in presenting the assets of a business, this can create some peculiar situations.

For example, there was a bank in Atlanta that had assets on its Balance Sheet called "Marketable Securities" (in other words, stocks) in an amount of approximately $77,000. In the notes to the Balance Sheet, which help explain where the numbers in the Balance Sheet come from, there was an item saying that "Marketable Securities includes stock of Coca Cola, Inc. purchased in 1917 ... with a current market value of $100,000,000." Would you say this bank's assets were a little understated on their balance sheet?

c.   Current Assets

Current assets are assets that you can use within 1 year.

Examples:

(1) CASH is something you can use anytime.

(2) ACCOUNTS RECEIVABLE are collected within a year (hopefully). "ALLOWANCE FOR DOUBTFUL ACCOUNTS" is an offset against Accounts Receivable where we estimate future bad debts.

(3) INVENTORY is sold within a year (hopefully). Inventory can include "raw materials" and "work-in-progress," as well as "finished goods." Each category is generally shown as a separate item within Inventory.

(4) PREPAID EXPENSES is where we put things we've paid for in advance until the item really comes due or is used up. The reason this account exists is that one of the key principles for our accounting system is "matching" in which we try to *match* expenses to the period they really belong in. Since an expense is a cost of operating your business for a particular period of time, you can actually pay for something that isn't an expense YET. For instance, you could pay a year's worth of insurance, but the expense is really incurred each month. Another example is a yearlong magazine subscription you prepay.

(5) SUPPLIES - Stationery, etc. that you use up quickly. If you have a restaurant or bar, they can also be things such as napkins and straws.

d. Fixed Assets

"Fixed Assets" include things that are going to be around for more than a year.

    (1) Examples of fixed assets are:

        (a) LAND

        (b) BUILDINGS

        (c) EQUIPMENT

        (d) NOTES RECEIVABLE - Agreements under which someone owes you money and is paying over a period longer than 1 year.

        (e) MORTGAGES - The same as a Notes Receivable except you have some real property (land and/or buildings) as collateral.

    (2) Buildings, other real property (land, etc.) and equipment are NOT inventory if you're not in the business of buying and selling such items. Even though you could sell them if you wanted to, such sales would not be in the "normal course of your business" and, therefore, it is presumed they'll last and that you're going to keep them for more than a year.

    (3) Depreciation is the means by which you take a portion of an item's cost and expense it over a certain period of time.

    Let's say you bought a computer for $1000 cash and used it all year in your business. Remembering the principal of "matching," the entire cost of buying a computer is not an expense in the tear you bought it because the computer is something you'll have for more than 1 year. So you say, "But having that computer is an expense of my business and I should be able to take that as expense deduction on my taxes." At the same time, a bank looking at your financial statements would say, "You've had that computer for a year and it's not worth $1000." So how do you deal with these comments, both of which are right? The answer is "depreciation."

Using the "straight-line" method of depreciation, you take the $1000 cost and divide by the number of years it will last (5). Your depreciation expense for that computer each year is $200.

The total of all the depreciation taken on property you still own is called "Accumulated Depreciation" and appears on The Balance Sheet, while the depreciation expense is on the Income Statement. If the computer were your only equipment, the "Equipment" section of your Balance Sheet would look like the following at the end of each of the 5 years you take depreciation. (You can't take more depreciation than your cost. So, in years after #5, the Equipment section would be the same as in Year 5 if you didn't make any new purchases.)

Note in the following example, as in most financial presentations, a number in parentheses or in brackets means *minus* or *an offset.*

	Yr 1	Yr 2	Yr 3	Yr 4
Equipment	$1000	$1000	$1000	$1000
Less: Accumulated depreciation	($200)	($400)	($600)	($800)
Equipment, net of depreciation	$800	$600	$400	$200

Land is not depreciated because it doesn't wear out. It may slide, turn into mud, shake, rattle and roll (and you might have to write it off)...but under normal conditions, land doesn't wear out.

(4) Amortization is similar to depreciation except it applies to contracts, goodwill and other things that really aren't "things" but are evidence of some rights. For instance, if you bought a franchise, you might have the right to use someone's name in your business. If that franchise lasted for 10 years and you paid $10,000, you could take $1,000 per year in amortization expense ($10,000 divided by 10 years).

e. Current Liabilities

"Current Liabilities" are debts you're going to pay within 1 year.

Examples:

(1) ACCOUNTS PAYABLE are normal obligations to suppliers.

(2) PAYROLL PAYABLE includes salaries and wages which have been earned but not yet paid.

(3) SALES TAXES PAYABLE are sales taxes you've collected but have not turned over to the appropriate governmental agencies yet.

(4) EMPLOYMENT TAXES PAYABLE include withholding and other taxes.

(5) CUSTOMER DEPOSITS are liabilities because the money given to you hasn't been earned until you've done what you were supposed to -- whether it was to provide some services or deliver some goods. Until then, the customer is entitled to his or her money back; so it's liability. If the customer is not entitled to his money back, it does not have to be shown as a liability and can go directly into "Income."

(6) DEFERRED INCOME is a little tricky. Remember, again, that our accounting system is based on the principle that we try to match income and expenses with the period in which they're earned or expended. So, for instance, what happens

if someone pays you $300 in advance for 3 months services ($100 per month)? The journal entry would look like this:

Date	Description	Account	Debit	Credit
	Cash		$300	
	Deferred Income			$300

At the end of the first month, you would make this "adjusting" journal entry:

Date	Description	Account	Debit	Credit
	Deferred Income		$100	
	Income			$100

This "adjusting" entry shows that you've earned one month's worth of the money paid to you in advance. (The "Deferred Income" account is now $200, since you've debited a liability, which reduces it.)

f.   Current Portion of Long Term Debt

Current Portion of Long Term Debt is the part of your long term debt that is due within 1 year; such as the principal that will be paid on your 15 year mortgage within the next 12 months.

g   Long Term Liabilities

"Long Term Liabilities" extend for more than a year.

(1) NOTES PAYABLE are promissory notes saying you promise to pay someone sometime in the future.

(2) MORTGAGES are long term liabilities which have some "real property" (land and/or buildings) as collateral.

(3) BONDS are also a form of long term liability, sometimes with collateral and sometimes without (a company can have both at the same time).

h.   Equity

An explanation of the relative merits and meanings of the different kinds of equity is contained in the financing section of this book. This section deals only with how these accounts are reflected on the books and in the Balance Sheet.

Two kinds of stock you'll see are Common and Preferred. Common Stock represents the basic ownership of the company while Preferred Stock is given to people who get preferential treatment as to dividends and liquidation.

(1) COMMON STOCK generally has a "par" or "stated" value. Very often, you'll see Common Stock with a par or stated value of some small amount, say $1.00 or even $10; even though the price paid for that stock was more.

Example: ABC Inc. sells 10,000 shares of Common Stock which have a par value of $1 per share for $10,000

The journal entry would be:

Date	Description	Account	Debit	Credit
	Cash		$10,000	
	Common Stock			$1,000
	Capital Paid In Excess of Par			$9,000

You debit cash because you increased an asset (cash). You credit Common Stock because you increased your equity. Since the amount actually paid was greater than the par, you show the Common (or Capital Stock account as the par or stated value of the shares that were sold (10,000 shares at $10 per share) and the excess goes into an account called "Capital Paid In Excess of Par" ($10,000 - $9,000)

(2) PREFERRED STOCK also has a "par" value that is used as a base for figuring how much the company (1) must pay as a dividend and (2) can buy the stock back for.

For instance, preferred shareholders generally receive a fixed rate of dividends. ("Dividends" are distributions of profits to the shareholders.) The phrase "7% preferred stock" means the dividend is 7% of the par value.

Also, the company generally has a right to repurchase or "call" preferred stock. If the company can "call" at 110% of par, and the par value is $100, as it commonly is, the company could repurchase that stock for $110 per share.

If ABC Company sells 100 shares of $100 par value preferred stock, the journal entry would be:

Date	Description	Account	Debit	Credit
	Cash		$10,000	
	Preferred Stock			$10,000

Notice that the entry for the Preferred Stock is one line. This is because the amount paid for the stock equals the par value. Had the stock been sold for $150 per share, the journal entry would look like this:

Date	Description	Account	Debit	Credit
	Cash		$15,000	
	Preferred Stock			$10,000
	Capital Paid in Excess of Par			$5,000

(3) RETAINED EARNINGS is fairly easy to figure out. If "Earnings" is the amount the company has made or lost throughout its life, "Retained Earnings" is how much of that the business has kept. If the company has made profits of $100,000 and given dividends of $60,000 to its shareholders, the Retained Earnings account would be $40,000. If, on the other hand, the company had lost money, the Retained Earnings would be a negative number.

(4) TREASURY STOCK is a rare account for small businesses because it is stock that has been repurchased by the company and not canceled.

3.   The Income Statement

a. Definition

Unlike the Balance Sheet which looks at what you own and owe at a specific point in time, the Income Statement reflects the income you earned and what it cost to operate for a period of time, whether it be for a month or a year.

The sample financial statements use the calendar year, but businesses can have "fiscal" years which may be more appropriate for that business; such as a fiscal year ending June 30.

(1) REVENUES are what the business earned in selling its goods and services throughout the year. "Discounts, Returns and Allowances" are taken out to arrive at "Net Revenues" because these items are offsets against what came in, not an expense of generating that sale.

(2) COST OF GOODS SOLD is the cost of whatever you sold including the cost to purchase it, the cost to get it to you, any import duties and other costs that (a) relate directly to the item you sold and (b) you would not have paid for if you didn't sell that item. Cost of Goods Sold does not include sales commissions or office expense.

If you manufacture the item you sell, Cost of Goods Sold can include an allocation of the manufacturing overhead. For instance, if you use a machine that costs $100,000 and it can produce 100,000 widgets, you should include in your Cost of Goods Sold $1 per widget for use of that machine ($100,000 divided by the 100,000 unit capacity). The same kind of allocation can be based on a useful life limited by time, rather than by units.

Revenues less Cost of Goods Sold = Gross Profit. *It is critical to understand that when someone tells you "My gross profit is $100,000" that does not mean his business made money. Gross Profit does not include the expenses of operating the business, discussed below.*

(3) SALES, GENERAL AND ADMINISTRATIVE EXPENSES are the actual costs of running a business.

   (a) Expenses which exist even if you don't sell anything or which do not change with every little change in the amount of business you do are called *fixed* or *overhead*. Examples are rent and insurance.

   (b) Expenses that are directly related to the amount of business you do are *variable*, meaning that if you didn't do the business you wouldn't have the expense. An example is sales commissions.

   (c) Expenses that can be incurred - or not incurred - as a part of your business strategy are called *discretionary*, meaning that if you didn't pay it your business would still exist, although the level of your business might be affected. Examples are advertising, travel and entertainment.

(4) EARNINGS BEFORE INTEREST AND TAX is the difference between "Sales, General and Administrative Expenses." This is important because you want to be able to distinguish between this figure - what the business generates

- and the financing strategies that may affect interest and taxes that are included when figuring Net Income.

(5) EXTRAORDINARY ITEMS are those transactions or events that are not in the "normal course of business." For instance, assume you're in the business of repairing TV's and this year you sell the building your shop is in, which you bought 10 years ago for $10,000. The sale price was $100,000. Your profit would be $90,000 ($100,000 - $10,000).

It would not be accurate to say your business was more profitable. By separating this unusual or "extraordinary" transaction, you can keep track of your on-going business operations without distorting your business' performance.

4.   The Statement of Changes in Financial Position

Also called the "Statement of Sources and Uses of Funds," this tells you where your cash came from and where it went. You may ask "Isn't that my Income Statement?" It might be, and it might not be. The reason for this is that there are two ways to keep your books and records:

- Cash basis – If you keep your books on the cash basis, you record transactions only when you receive or pay cash. So, even if you did some work for someone, you record the transaction only when you get paid even if that's months later. If you use the cash basis, then the Income Statement and Statement of Changes in Financial Position will be the same.

- Accrual Basis – If you keep your books on the accrual basis, you record transactions when they occur. Unlike the above example where you did some work but didn't get paid for months, using the accrual basis you would have recorded as Accounts Receivable the amount you are to be paid. In this case, the Statement of Changes in Financial Position would be different because although you showed "income" from the work done, you did not actually get the cash.

If you recall from earlier in this book my recommendation:

THE KEY TO STARTING AND OPERATING A BUSINESS IS NOT PROFITS -- BUT CASH FLOW. "Profits" are NOT the same thing as cash ... and "profits" do you NO good if you don't have the cash to pay your bills!

a.   Sources of Funds

Some "sources" of money are fairly obvious, such as profits from your business or loans you take out. Why, though, do you add back Depreciation and "Increase (Decrease) in Accounts Payable"?

You add Depreciation back because it is not an expense that you actually put out cash for. As you can see in the "Uses" section, there's an item that says "Capital Expenditures." This is where the cost of buying, for instance, a piece of equipment ends up. Depreciation is simply a way of accounting for the periodic use of that asset - it's not something you pay cash for. Since you deducted it in getting to Net Income you have to add it back to determine how much cash you gained or lost in the year.

"Increase (Decrease) in Accounts Payable" is a trickier concept. Assume that all your accounts payable are for things you take as deduction - supplies, inventory you've sold, etc. What happens if you take a deduction but don't pay for it? You actually have more cash than is shown on your Income Statement. So, you should take out that amount to see how much cash you have. Therefore, if your accounts payable are $10 in one period and $20 the next, there are $10 more of expenses you deducted but didn't pay for, meaning you actually have $10 more cash than your Net Income figure would suggest. The opposite would be true if your accounts payable declined; meaning you paid more accounts payable than you took deductions for and you would, therefore, deduct the amount of the decrease in your accounts payable from your sources.

(Alternatively, you could add to Uses a decrease in Accounts Payable... but that is a decision for you and your accountant to make.)

b.   Uses

Under Uses, "Increase (Decrease) in Accounts Receivable" is the other side of the discussion above. If you record a sale but don't collect the cash, you've increased your Net Income but haven't improved your cash. So, if your accounts receivable go up, you count the increase as a "Use" of funds. Again, the opposite is that if your accounts receivable go down, that means you have collected more cash than you recorded as sales from new accounts receivable. (Alternatively, you could add to Sources a decrease in Accounts Receivable ... but that is a decision for you and your accountant to make.)

5.   Ratio Analysis

Ratios and statistical analyses don't tell everything about a business. However, they do give some standard measures to use in evaluating your or someone else's business. For instance, if you know that the average profit margin percentage (Net Income/Net Sales) in a given industry is 12% and yours is 15%, you know you're doing better than the industry average. Consequently, the following ratios don't mean much except in comparison to some standard or norm. In that context, they are figures that are relied on greatly by banks, investors and managers alike.

As you read the following, you may wonder what the difference is between "Sales" and "Net Sales." A simple way to explain is by example: If I sell you 2 hats for $25 each, my sales are $50. But if you come back and show me that one of the hats is damaged, and I give you back $5, my *net sales* (i.e., my sales after "returns, discounts and allowances") are $45 -- not $50.

- Gross Profit Margin Percent = Gross Profit ÷ Net Sales x 100

- Contribution Margin = Net Sales - Variable Cost

- Contribution Margin Percentage = (Net Sales - Variable Cost) ÷ Net Sales x 100

- Net Profit Margin Percentage = Net Income after Taxes ÷ Net Sales x 100

- Current Ratio = Current Assets ÷ Current Liabilities

- Quick Ratio (Current Assets - Inventory) ÷ Current Liabilities

- Accounts Receivable Turnover = Sales on Credit ÷ Accounts Receivable

- Days Sales in Receivable = Receivables x (Credit Sales / 360)

- Inventory Turnover = Sales ÷ Inventory

- Days Sales in Inventory = Inventory ÷ (Sales / 360)

- Debt Ratio = Total Liabilities ÷ Total Assets

- Debt-to-Equity Ratio = Total Liabilities ÷ Total Equity

- Debt Coverage Ratio = (Net Income + Interest) ÷ (Debt Principal + Interest Payments)

- Return on Assets Percentage = Net Income ÷ Total Assets x 100

- Return on Equity = Net Income ÷ Total Equity x 100

- Return on Investment = Net Income ÷ (Equity - Retained Earnings) x 100

C. ISSUES

As mentioned at the beginning of this chapter, there are many choices you can make related to accounting. Some have been discussed already but will be briefly mentioned here again. There are many other issues and many complex aspects of the issues below which are beyond the scope of this book. You should consult an accountant or business consultant for more details.

1. Financial vs. Tax Reporting

Many businesses have two sets of books: one for financial reporting purposes and one for tax purposes. (Did you think I meant something else by "two sets of books"?) The books for financial reporting purposes are what you are primarily concerned with, since that's where the financial statements come from. The tax books are for the Internal Revenue Service and other taxing agencies. Tax returns are also used by lenders when "audited" financial statements are not available. There are differences between the two sets of books which affect the amount of taxes you actually pay.

2. Cash Basis vs. Accrual Basis Accounting

"Cash basis" is a term used to describe the method of accounting. The alternative to "cash basis" is "accrual basis." A business using the cash basis shows income and expenses only when it gets or pays money. A business using the accrual basis shows income and expenses as soon as it is *entitled* to money or *owes* it.

Example: Assume your dentist performs services for you and sends you a bill. That same dentist then buys some supplies on credit.

A dentist using the cash basis wouldn't show any income until you pay your bill. The accrual basis dentist shows income as soon as he/she bills you.

A dentist using the cash basis wouldn't show any expense for the supplies until he/she pays the bill. The accrual basis dentist shows expenses as soon as he/she is billed by the supplier.

So what? First, under US tax laws (and similar laws of other clountries), if you have inventory you <u>must</u> use the accrual method, so the choice isn't there.

But if you do have a choice, here's the difference it makes:

Assume the dentist rendered those services to you in December of Year 1 and you didn't pay the bill until next May Year 2. Since the cash basis dentist only reports income when cash is received, he didn't put it on his Year 1 tax return so he didn't pay tax on money he didn't get yet. The accrual basis dentist, though, reported the income and paid tax on April 15, Year 2 for money he didn't get until May.

That doesn't sound good, but the expense side is where the difference really counts. The accrual basis dentist who reports a deduction for the expenses in December Year 1 but doesn't pay the bill until May Year 2 has actually taken a deduction for an amount he hasn't paid. The cash basis dentist can't take the deduction until he actually pays the bill.

You may think this can give you a real windfall, but the reality is that if you operate consistently not just from Year 1 to Year 2, but then to Years 3, 4, 5 and so on, it evens itself out so there is not as much difference as it may first appear.

3. Depreciation Methods

There are different methods of depreciation which can be used. With the "straight-line" method you simply divide your cost ("basis") by how long the asset will last (its useful life). There is also "accelerated depreciation" which gives you more depreciation in the first few years than in the later years.

You can choose either for financial reporting purposes and choose a different one for tax purposes. What difference do these choices make?

Example: You buy a machine for $10,000 with a useful life of 10 years, and it will be worth nothing at the end of that period. Your net income before taxes, not including depreciation is $20,000; and your only asset is the machine.

- STRAIGHT LINE DEPRECIATION is $1,000 per year ($10,000/10). If you use straight line for financial reporting and tax purposes, you would have net income for financial reporting and tax purposes of $19,000. Your total assets would be $9,000 ($10,000-$1,000 depreciation).

- ACCELERATED DEPRECIATION ("Double Declining Balance" is one example of accelerated depreciation) is $2,000 in the first year. If you used accelerated depreciation for both financial and tax purpose, your net income for financial and tax purposes would be $18,000. So you'd pay less income taxes in for Year 1; but your total assets are only $8,000.

- If, however, you used straight line for financial purposes and accelerated for tax purposes, you would pay tax on only $18,000 but could still show investors and bankers net income of $19,000 and total assets of $9,000.

4.   Inventory Methods

There are different methods which can, in times of fluctuating prices, have an enormous impact on your financial statements. Unlike depreciation, however, whichever method you choose must be used for both financial reporting and tax purposes.

Example: You sell lots of widgets, but very few of Model A, which are imported from Japan. You generally like to have three in stock, but you now have only two. You bought Widget #1 two years ago for $100 and you bought Widget #2 one year ago for $120. Now you want to buy another to get your stock back up to three units. Since you bought Widget #2, prices have gone way up. Widget #3 will cost you $200. A customer then calls and wants to buy a Model A widget, which you sell for $300.

The inventory method you choose will determine whether you have a cost of $100, $120 or $200.

The accounts that will be affected are Cost of Goods Sold (on the Income Statement) and Inventory (on the Balance Sheet). Sales will not be affected because the sale price is $300 no matter which widget you take out of inventory. The following are three scenarios using different inventory methods:

a.   Perpetual Inventory/Specific Identification Method

With this method, you use the cost that you paid for the specific widget you sold. The following chart illustrates the different accounts depending on which widget you sold. The Beginning Inventory is the total of what you have paid for all your widgets, or $420 ($100 + $120 + $200).

	Widget #1	Widget #2	Widget #3
Beginning Inventory	$420	$420	$420
Sales	$300	$300	$300
Cost of Goods Sold	$100	$120	$200
GROSS PROFIT	$200	$180	$100
Ending Inventory	$320	$300	$220

As you can see, by selling Widget #1 you have:

a. The highest gross profit, which is good for financial reporting purposes -- good for creditors and shareholders;

b. The highest taxable income, meaning the highest tax to pay; and

c. The highest inventory, which gives you more total assets -- can be good for creditors (too much inventory may be bad because it may indicate you are holding things you can't sell), but can also mean higher taxes because many states impose a periodic tax on inventories.

By selling Widget #3 you have:

a. The lowest gross profit;

b. The lowest taxable income, meaning the lowest tax to pay; and

c. The lowest inventory, which gives you less total assets.

Widget #2 is in the middle.

b.   First-In/First Out (FIFO) Method

This means that no matter which widget you actually take from inventory and sell, the cost you use is the cost of the *oldest one (i.e., the first one you bought and still have)* in inventory. So, you would automatically take the cost from Widget #1.

The choice is important because different people have different goals. If, in times of rising prices, it's more important for you to impress investors or lenders than to reduce your taxable income, you would probably choose FIFO. The results would be opposite, however, if instead of prices rising they fell.

c.   Last-in/Last-out (LIFO) Method

No matter which widget you actually take from inventory and sell, you use the cost of the *last one* you purchased. Your results would be the same as those indicated for #3 above. Notice that when prices are rising, this gives you the lowest taxable income and is good for a business that does not have to impress lenders or investors because it conserves cash. Again, the results would be different if prices were falling rather than rising.

5.   Certified Audits

A "certified audit" is an audit performed by a certified public accountant within certain parameters and criteria. The key to the value of a certified audit is that the CPA is supposed to be independent of the firm that is being audited. This gives management, lenders and investors a greater feeling of comfort that the financial statements fairly present the financial picture of the company without the bias that company management might have.

A certified audit costs significantly more than financial statements prepared by management, which are unaudited. Why, then, should you get audited statements?

1. Audited statements are often required by loan agreements.

2. Audited statements are often required by outside investors.

3. The process of being audited by an outside party helps assure you and others of the integrity of your reporting systems and/or personnel.

4. Audited statements are almost always required to *go public* (i.e., sell your company's shares on a public market). If you can't afford it right away, be aware that prior to any sale, you will probably have to go back for three years and audit the statements. Good records will help keep costs down later.

6.   Outsides Accountants

A bookkeeper, full or part time, probably can give you what you need; at least at the start. However, an outside accountant is not always more expensive. Consider the following:

1. An outside accountant might cost you more per hour, but he/she might be much faster and do a lot more for you than an in-house bookkeeper; and

2. An outside accountant will maintain your records in a way that will make filing tax returns easier and, even if your statements are not audited, make a later certified audit easier and less expensive.

VI.   FINANCE

Accounting deals with the record keeping process and choices that affect that process. Finance deals with where you get your money, on what terms and what you do with it.

A.   TYPE OF FINANCING

1.   Equity

Equity is the owners' capital; meaning that this investment goes in with no promise of getting anything back. Why say "capital" instead of "money"? Because while *capital* certainly can include money, it can also include other things that have a value to your business, such as property, equipment, patents and other things. Consequently, we use capital because it is a convenient word to cover all possible items that could be invested in your business.

Equity is what you, as the entrepreneur, will be getting for your capital investment. No matter how optimistic you are about the prospects of the new business, anyone - you or outside investors - investing in the equity of the business must understand that this investment could be lost. You don't have to like it, but you do have to understand that it can happen.

Following are some typical forms of equity.

Sine a sole proprietorship is you, you are the owner. Even if you file a fictitious business statement, also known as a "DBA" (doing business as), it's still you. So, the money is yours but should, to make accounting easier, be kept in separate accounts.

A partnership is you and one or more other people or entities. The owners are called "partners." The interests are generally called "partnership interests" or "partnership units."

If a corporation and a partnership had children, they would be either a limited liability company or a limited a partnership, both with attributes of a corporation and a partnership.

- In a limited liability company, the owners are called "members," the member that is running the business is called the "managing member" and the equity interests are called "membership units."

- In a limited partnership, the owners are called "limited partners," the partner that is running the business is called the "general partner" and the equity interests are called "partnership units."

In a corporation, the owners are called "stockholders" or "shareholders." The shareholders elect a Board of Directors who, in turn, elect the top management of the corporation. The equity interests are called "stock" or "shares." Unlike other forms of organization, corporations can have different kinds of shares, giving the organization a lot of flexibility in structuring the investments and rights of owners. Following is a description of a few and the differences between them.

If a corporation offers so much flexibility, why would anyone choose another form of organization? Because there may be other issues such as taxation, liability and transferability that are more important than being able to create different classes of shareholders. This is one of those areas where you now know there are questions to be asked before you begin your business.

a. Common Stock

Common stock (shares) represents the basic ownership interests of a corporation. Any number of shares can be authorized in the Articles of Incorporation (filed with the state in which the company is created) and issued to shareholders, who are then the owners of the business.

As discussed in the Accounting chapter, common stock is assigned a "par" or "stated" value. This does not limit what the shares can be sold for. A share of common stock with a par value of $.01 could be sold for $1000; the excess going into the "Capital Paid In Excess of Par" account.

Unless otherwise stated, each share of common stock is given one vote, with the majority of the shares controlling. Shareholders do not manage the day-to-day business of the company. Shareholders normally vote on things such as electing the Board of Directors, changing the Articles, acquiring another business or selling out and other things that affect the basic nature of the business. In other words, there doesn't have to be a shareholder vote for every decision that occurs.

While each share of common stock generally has one vote, this does not have to be the case. Sometimes a corporation that wants to give different shareholders proportionately equal ownership of the company but not equal control will create different classes of common stock.

> Example: John started ABC Company. He has three children who are working equally with him and he's willing to share the company equally but he doesn't want there to be any question who the boss is. If John were to issue 1000 common shares equally to himself and his 3 children, each would have 250 shares, or 25% of the outstanding shares; and his three children could get together and out vote him. Instead, John issues himself 250 shares of Class A common stock and he gives his children 750 shares of Class B common stock. He and his children still own the company equally (25% each), but Class A common stock has four votes per share while Class B common stock has only one vote per share. This gives John 1000 votes and his children 750, so John has the majority of the total 1750 possible votes and control of ABC Company.

b.   Preferred Stock

Preferred stock is, as you might guess, stock that gets preferred or better treatment than common stock. As with most things in life, however, there are pluses and minuses. Some of the characteristics of preferred stock are described below.

Dividends

If the company has profits, preferred shareholders must get their dividends before the common shareholders get theirs. Preferred dividends are generally fixed at a percentage of the *par* value – a value that can be set by management. For instance, if the preferred stock had a par value of $100 per share, then "7% preferred stock" of this company would be entitled to $7 per share annual dividends *before* the common shareholders could get anything.

Since the Board of Directors has the discretion to declare and pay dividends - or not - what happens if there's a profit and the Board of Directors chooses not to pay a dividend one year?

If the preferred stock is *cumulative*, unpaid dividends just keep adding up so that all the unpaid dividends for past years ("dividends in arrears") as well as for the current year must be paid before the common shareholders can receive any dividends.

If the preferred stock is *non-cumulative*, any dividends not paid to the preferred shareholders are lost, but any current dividends must be paid to the preferred shareholders before common shareholders can get any dividends.

Example: In addition to its common shares, XYZ Company has $100,000 of 5% *non*-cumulative preferred stock outstanding; therefore, the annual dividend on the preferred stock is $5,000. Last year, net profits (meaning after taxes) were $6,000 and this year net profits were $7,000.

- If the preferred shareholders had gotten dividends last year and this year, they would have received $5,000 each year, leaving $1,000 for the common shareholders last year and $2,000 this year. Preferred shareholders would, therefore, have received a two-year total of $10,000 while common shareholders would have received $3,000.

- If the Board of Directors declared no dividends for preferred shareholders last year and, therefore, no dividends to common shareholders, waiting until this year to declare the whole $13,000 as dividends, the preferred shareholders would get their $5,000 and the common shareholders *could* get $8,000 ($5,000 more by deferring declaration of the dividend 1 year).

If preferred stock were cumulative, the unpaid $5,000 dividend from last year would carry over and have to be paid when dividends are declared.

Voting Rights

Preferred stock generally has no voting rights except as to issues that directly affect the nature of their investment. Some preferred stock, however, has a provision that if no dividend is declared for a certain number of periods, the preferred stockholders acquire new rights, such as voting rights. Often, under such provisions, the voting rights acquired by the preferred shareholders are enough to give the preferred shareholders control of the business.

Convertibility

Sometimes, preferred stock is *convertible* into common stock. This means that each share of preferred stock can be exchanged at the option of the preferred shareholder for a specified number of common shares or at a specified value. The preferred shareholder might do this if preferred stock was purchased because the buyer felt it was safer than common stock and later saw that the returns would be higher with common stock.

Example: Three years ago, you bought $10,000 of 10% cumulative convertible preferred stock in ABC Company (i.e., a $1,000 annual dividend on your stock). ABC has never missed a dividend. Now, the company is doing well and your preferred stock is convertible into 5000 shares of common stock on which there is no dividend. However, in the last year the common stock has doubled in price from $.75 to $1.50 per share. Your right to convert your preferred stock is about to expire, so here's your choice:

- Keep your $1,000 per year dividend (on which you're paying income tax) and the preferred stock which will never be worth much more than $10,000; OR

- Trade your preferred stock for which you paid $10,000 for common stock presently worth $7,500 with no dividend. If the stock keeps going up in price the way it has, the stock could be worth $15,000 in another year and $ 25,000 a year after that.

Classes

Like common stock, there can be more than one class of preferred stock, usually with different dividend rates, convertibility features and other attributes.

Callability

One of the features of preferred stock which is positive from the business' point of view and negative from the investor's is that preferred stock is often "callable." This means that the company that issued the stock has an option to buy back the preferred stock at an agreed premium (the "call premium").

Example: ABC Company issues 7% preferred stock, $100 par, with a 10% call premium. This means that ABC can buy back that preferred stock for $110 - 10% more than par. The impact on the investor is that this puts a ceiling on the price to which the stock will rise, because why would anyone pay $125 for a share of preferred stock that the company could at any time buy back $110?

Liquidation

If the shareholders - including owners of preferred stock - decide to shut the business down and liquidate it, preferred shareholders get their par value back before common shareholders get anything, but after the creditors (if there's anything left to get at that point).

2. Debt

A debt is, of course, when you owe someone something, usually money. What many people don't know is that there is an almost infinite variety of ways to structure debt.

An issue that goes beyond the scope of this book is the *after-tax cost* of the various types of financing. Dividends on common and preferred stock are not tax deductible while interest on debt is. This makes a big difference and should be looked at closely.

a. Unsecured Loan

(1) An unsecured loan is when a lender, maybe a bank but more likely for an entrepreneur a friend or relative, lends you money in exchange for only your promise to pay back (the same as a credit card). The lender is relying on your honesty. Of course, the lender, before agreeing to make that kind of loan, is also going to rely on your ability to repay the loan. As an individual, institutional lenders (such as a bank) rely on your credit score. As a business, lenders will look at your assets and income. If the business is new, a sole proprietorship, a general partnership or a limited partnership of which you're the general partner, the lender will look at your personal credit score and assets as well as those of the business and probably require you to personally guarantee the loan. This means that if the business doesn't pay the loan, you will.

(2) A not uncommon feature is the lender's requirement that you maintain a *compensating* or minimum balance in a non-interest bearing or low interest account at their institution.

Example: First National Bank of Bernard lends you $10,000 at 8% annual interest which you agree to pay back in one year. The total amount you would pay, including interest, will be $10,800. The bank could say it wants you to keep a compensating balance of $2,000 in your checking account, which is $1,000 more than you would normally keep in that account. In this case, you don't have the use of $10,000 since $1,000 was taken out of circulation by remaining in your account. Your loan, then, was effectively only $9,000, yet you still have to pay $800 in interest (8% on 10,000). The effective interest rate is, therefore, almost 9% ($800/$9000).

Since compensating balances make your effective interest payment higher, you should figure it out and base your decision on the *effective* interest rate, not on the *stated rate*.

(3) When you create a large amount of debt and make it available in pieces so that, possibly, many people can "invest" in your debt, this is called a "bond." The contract defining the rights of the borrower and the lenders is called the "debenture."

(4) Another type of unsecured loan which people generally don't think about is your *accounts payable*. When a supplier sells you goods or services and you have 30 days to pay, that's an unsecured loan.

b.   Secured Loan

   (1) A secured loan is when the creditor has some collateral. The collateral can be any asset you have. The creditor could require:

      (a) A certain amount of cash to be placed in a certificate of deposit (like a long term savings account).

      (b) A lien be placed on real property you own (like a home loan) so that if you don't pay they can take over the property and/or sell it to pay the debt. (The creditor in this case would then have either a mortgage or a trust deed on your property. The difference between the two is principally in the method of enforcement, the specifics of which are beyond the scope of this program; but can be important if you have one. So, ask.)

      (c) A lien be placed on personal property you own (equipment, furniture or inventory) so that if you don't pay they can take over the property and/or sell it to pay the debt. A bond can also be secured by personal property. In the context of business assets as collateral, this particular kind of lien is commonly referred to in the US (except Louisiana) as a "UCC-1," which is the form filed with the county clerk where the property is located.

      (d) Accounts receivable be assigned to the creditor so that the people who owe you money will pay the creditor, thereby reducing your loan. This kind of financing is generally used as a "revolving" credit, meaning the borrower always needs some credit because he has to get the money from his sales faster than his customers generally pay. Many industries such as the garment business use this form of financing extensively which is also called *factoring*.

(2) Similarly to preferred stock, the business can make debt convertible into a certain number of shares of a designated class of stock. For an example of convertible bonds, review the example under preferred stock, and just imagine the preferred stock is debt and instead of the holder receiving a dividend, it's interest.

B.   SOURCES OF FINANCING

In theory there are many sources of financing for new businesses. The reality, though, does not always seem to bear that out.

1.   Your Own Money

a.   Before committing your own resources, consider several factors:

(1) People who have never started their own business before, and even many people who have, drastically underestimate the amount of money that will really be needed.

Example: You project your sales to be $10,000 per month. You sell on 30 day credit but 60% of your customers don't pay for 60 days, another 30% don't pay for 90 days, 5% don't pay for 120 days and the last 5% don't pay at all. Your budgeted expenses are $3,000 per month and the cost of what you sold (what you have to pay your suppliers) is $5,000. Assuming you have to pay your suppliers up front, you're going to need $6,000 just to cover your operating expenses for 60 days until you get paid by most of your customers. If you had figured $10,000 sale less $5,000 cost of goods sold leaves you $5,000 to pay expenses (so, therefore, you don't need any more money for operating) you would have been wrong, broke and probably out of business within three months.

(2) Do you have enough capital to sustain yourself, your family and the business for a long enough period to let the business get established?

(3) What will the impact be on you and your family if the business does not succeed?

    (a) Will you be financially able to provide the basic needs of your family?

    (b) Will you be psychologically affected if the business does not succeed such that you will be a different person than the one you, your family and friends have become accustomed to and love?

2.   Family and Friends

This is both an easy and a difficult source of financing.

a.   It's easy because:

(1) They're people you know.

(2) They're people who know you.

(3) They're people who, for the most part, you can trust.

(4) They're people who, for the most part, care about you and your success, which would be a reason for providing some capital that outsiders wouldn't.

b.   It's difficult because:

(1) They feel bad saying "no" and, therefore, are under a lot of pressure when you ask. They may say "yes" to not hurt your feelings; but back out when it comes time to actually give you money, which then makes you feel bad because you feel betrayed or misled. Other times they may back off from the relationship rather than say "no." It's a good way to lose friends and alienate family.

(2) If the business does not succeed and the capital is lost, one or more of the following may occur:

    (a) You'll feel guilty and this will affect your relationship.

(b)   They'll feel bad and this will affect the relationship. If they gave you a loan, they'll feel bad asking for the money back and you may react by asking them to forgive the loan or change the terms you agreed to; again affecting the relationship.

(c)   They will use the relationship as a basis for pressuring you to pay them back even if they invested in the equity as opposed to making you a loan, saying something like, "I wouldn't have done it if we weren't friends, so now I expect you to act like a friend and give me my money back." First, that is not someone who is a friend and not a feeling you need to deal with. Assuming you've been up front, honest and told the people what they're getting into (including the risks), they're not entitled to anything; but that won't stop them from asking.

c.   A word to the wise:

No matter how close a friend, do not take money from an attorney unless you know for a fact that he or she has invested in other start-up businesses, lost some money and did NOT sue the entrepreneurs. The reason for this warning is that a vindictive attorney can sue you with little cost to him or herself, knowing that even if he or she loses it will cause you a great deal of expense and anxiety. Having said that, the pressures of raising capital are enormous and it is very difficult to turn down financing when it's offered, no matter who it's from. So, at least try to get financing from people other than a friend and other than an attorney. (In case you did not read my bio, I'm an attorney. So, no offense intended to the vast majority of good attorneys.)

3.   Independent Brokers

Independent brokers can be a tremendous help since it's their business to know where to get financing. A broker is, in fact, anyone who puts a buyer and a seller together. The biggest problem from an entrepreneur's point of view is that anyone can call him or herself a broker and make claims and promises. When you start counting on them to perform, you're usually left disappointed, several months down the road with nothing to show for it, and possibly quite a bit of money lighter because you began preparing for the launch too soon (like by leaving your job).

BE CAREFUL OF BROKERS WHO ASK YOU FOR MONEY UP FRONT. Brokers get paid by commission for being successful. Someone who wants to get paid even if they fail should be looked at carefully. Some well-known accounting and law firms may want a fee and some firms may want an advance against out of pocket expenses. You simply have to evaluate your chances of success with each channel, get the opinion of an objective third party and ask for references of satisfied customers.

Unlike the "friend or family" situation described above, dealing with an attorney who is a business finance broker is an easier relationship for 2 reasons:

1. If they or their contacts provide financing, it's because they have made a conscious business decision and understand the risks; not because of their friendship with you.

2. If providing financing to businesses, particularly new businesses, is something the attorney does on a regular basis, he or she most likely understands the nature and risks inherent in such activities and looks at it much more realistically (even fatalistically), rather than taking it personally as would an attorney/friend (or ex-friend).

4.   Traditional Brokerage Firms

Don't go to a traditional brokerage firm.

When you think of a traditional broker, you might think of Goldman Sachs, JP Morgan or Merrill Lynch. Brokers can be members of firms or they can be individuals operating as independents.

While there are exceptions to every rule, there are so few exceptions to this rule that you can be very confident of it: If you've got a startup business, DON'T WASTE YOUR TIME GOING TO MAJOR BROKERAGE FIRMS. Unless you've got the cure for a major disease or the secret to anti-gravity, they won't provide financing for you because:

a.   Due to the inherent risks in start-ups, there is too great a possibility of suit by the investors and liability in the event of failure.

b.   The costs associated with going through a major brokerage are extremely high; which could be more than the money you need to start your business.

c.   The amount of work a major brokerage needs to do to put your deal into its system is similar to the amount of work they have to do to put a $250,000,000 deal in. At a commission rate of 3%, they can earn $7.5 million on the other deal or 3% of your deal. Which would you do?

5.   Venture Capital Companies

This may be one of the most inappropriate and misleading names I've heard. You would think that the business of venture capital companies ("VC's") is helping to launch good ideas and new businesses; and that's what many will tell you their business.

The truth is that most (not all) venture capital companies want to provide expansion capital to businesses that (a) have been in existence for at least three years and (b) want to expand or make an acquisition. Some VC's will provide capital to businesses that have been in existence but are losing money with the potential to turn around. A smaller portion of VC's provide financing to start-ups; which is the only kind of venture capital company you're concerned with at this point.

Some broad characteristics of venture capital companies are:

- They want equity; potentially a fairly large amount.
- Some act as brokers while others invest their own or clients' money.

- Some focus on certain geographical areas or industries.
- They usually look for an exit in three to five years with a 5-10 times return on investment.

If a venture capital company is helping to launch an untested idea, it's entitled to a high return from the ones that succeed in order to pay for all those ideas they invested in that didn't and won't succeed. The high return gives them the incentive to keep investing in new ideas, knowing that many will fail.

Another important factor to VC's is HOW TO GET OUT – aka the "exit strategy." Keeping in mind that an investment can be profitable because of either the income it generates or its appreciation in value, a VC's primary interest is the latter. The ways to realize that appreciation are to either go public (sell stock to the public) or just sell the VC's interest. If your business doesn't have excellent growth potential, a VC is most likely not going to be your financier; even though you and your family might be very happy with the income to be earned over a long period of time.

In order that you don't spend your time and money in vain, do your homework by researching each venture capital company you are considering. Try to understand what each VC is going to look for and to match what you have with the one(s) that are consistent, if any. Don't, for instance, call a VC specializing in medical technology with an idea for a new retail store or vice versa.

Too often, the first person you speak to at a VC will not really understand what you're saying or even what the VC is doing. They may tell you to send a business plan and whatever drawings and samples you have, even though there is no realistic possibility of that VC doing anything with you other than getting your hopes up. They don't do that intentionally but a person imagines the best possible outcome unless given a clear and outright rejection. If you haven't already researched that firm yourself, do so, check out their website and ask the firm for some information about the firm and its investments. You can get a good idea from that whether your project will be in the ballpark.

6.   Banks

This category of sources is very easy to explain:

a.   Banks do not invest in startups.

b.   Banks lend money to people based on their personal credit and assets. If you have a home with equity, many banks will lend you money for your new business using your home as collateral. That's nothing special, though, since you could take that money and buy a boat or go on a great vacation. It often doesn't matter to the bank what you use the money for since they have your house as security.

7.   Small Business Administration ("SBA") Loans

Contrary to what many people think, the SBA does not lend money. The SBA *guarantees loans* made by banks to people starting new businesses. If you don't pay the loan, the SBA loan will pay and then come looking for you.

Applying for an SBA loan is a somewhat long and complex process; but often very valuable. There are people experienced in processing these applications who can help (for a fee).

8.   Related Businesses

Related businesses are companies which may be doing the exact same thing you're doing or are in a supporting or related field. For instance, if you've got an idea for a new widget with some amazing new twists, you could go to an existing manufacturer of widgets or you could go to companies that distribute widgets or even a major user of widgets that would benefit from your new design.

DIRECTLY RELATED BUSINESSES are companies that are presently in the same business as you're contemplating. The advantages of working with such a company is that they know your business, can help overcome obstacles and can provide expertise and maybe distribution, marketing or other elements you are missing. Sounds logical, right?

The disadvantage is that they can also do it themselves. Why give you ownership in something they can have their own employees do? For this reason, it is critical to have a written agreement with the company before telling them your idea that they will not use it for their own benefit or tell anyone else. This is commonly called a "Non-Disclosure Agreement" or "NDA."

The problem with NDA's is that many large companies will not sign them out of fear that they are already working on something similar and do not want to jeopardize their own projects. Additionally, what do you do if you feel that a large company that did sign your NDA has violated it? You have the right to hire an attorney, to sue, to spend a lot of money and maybe, if you're still alive, win ... and then they can appeal.

You may be much better off going to them after you've started and gotten to a point where it would be too obvious if they simply stole your work ... and you could more easily win in court or cause them public relations damage.

SUPPLIERS would seem to be a logical source of capital. It makes sense to go to a company and say, "We're going to be a big customer and if you give us the money to start we'll buy all our product from you." The problem is that they've heard it before and it almost never actually happens. Still, once in a while a supplier will see something they believe in and someone might say "yes." Still, most will say "no" for two reasons:

- The supplier has to lay out money for material and labor. The supplier may not have the credit for the materials; and the supplier's employees certainly aren't going to wait until you get your money. A big company has the resources, but your best bet would probably be a well-financed small company that's hungry for business.

- Since the money is being paid by your customer to you, there is a chance that you won't pay the supplier. The supplier would then be out the money the supplier spent on labor and materials as well as its profit. This is especially true for foreign manufacturers who may want a "letter of credit" ("LC") for the full purchase price before they make your product. A letter of credit is a bank's promise to pay on your behalf so you don't have to put up the cash yourself. Since a well-known bank's promise is easier to collect on than a small business' or an individual's, foreign manufacturers take the letter of credit which the supplier then tries to borrow on ... in theory.

The reality is that for a bank to issue a letter of credit on your behalf, they want to know that you'll pay so you will probably have to deposit with the bank cash in the amount of the letter of credit or take out a personal loan secured by collateral.

If you have to put up the cash to get the LC, is there any benefit to using a letter of credit? The advantage is that the terms of the LC generally provide that the supplier gets paid only when the goods are delivered to a shipper or the U.S., so at least you haven't lost control of your money and been forced to go chase a supplier in another country.

The advantages of working with suppliers are:

- They know what you're talking about.

- They know the risks involved.

- They have existing facilities and channels that you might be able to plug directly into, thereby jumping over a lot of the obstacles ordinarily encountered in starting a new business. This enables you to focus on your skills, whether they be sales, manufacturing, creative or something else, rather than deal with personnel, accounting, landlords, payroll, etc.

The disadvantages are:

- They know when you don't know what you're talking about.

- They may want complete ownership of the project, as opposed to making a passive investment.

- They could do it themselves. If they say "no"' there's someone else who knows your idea. What if one of many people at that company later decides it's a good idea... without you? This is why you have to be careful about protecting an idea that can be copied and why, sometimes, you choose not to approach some of the most obvious sources for financing. As discussed in the Law chapter, patents, copyrights and trademarks are fine, but the main thing they give you is a right to sue in court and, maybe, after many years of legal fighting and thousands of dollars of cost, win. On the other hand, you might lose. Most big companies don't need or want the headache or bad press associated with being sued for stealing someone's idea. But sometimes it happens, even by accident. (See discussion of "Confidentiality Agreements" in the Law section.)

VII.   LAW

You should know by now that the goal of this book is not to know all the answers but to ask the right questions. That goal is especially true in this chapter where there is so much information. Again, you may wonder why you should know any of this – You can call an attorney whenever you have a question, right? It's right if you have a lot of money to spend on lawyers.

The reality is that the issues discussed below impact you on a daily basis; and your budget probably does not include money to have an attorney sitting next to you all day long or on retainer (unless he or she is a friend and you've offered some equity in the business – which is a possibility). In any case, it's better to have a basic understanding of the legal environment in which you will operate and to recognize when there's an issue for which you really need legal assistance.

Also, *having* certain rights can be very different than *enforcing* them. This is like going through an intersection, having the right of way, seeing someone else running the stop light and instead of stopping you think "I have my rights" and you get into an accident.

Know your rights, but always consider the practical implications of enforcing your rights – what will it cost in terms of time, effort, money, reputation.

A.   CONTRACTS

1.   Introduction

There are two basic legal systems in the western world: *common law* and *civil law*. In the common law system, the applicable rules are developed over a period of time based on precedent (i.e., what's come before). In the civil law system, every case fits into a law or statute; and there is never any question whether there is a rule that will apply, only which rule applies.

Most of Europe, for example, uses civil law; while the United States, United Kingdom and Australia use common law (except Louisiana which carries its French traditions by using civil law). However, as more rules are set out in statutes and regulations by federal, state and local governments and agencies, the common law system we have in the US is acquiring more of the characteristics of civil law.

In the United States, we have both federal and state laws. Many countries have only one level of laws. So, to reduce or try to eliminate potential conflicts and confusion, one set of rules adopted by all states in the US (except Louisiana) is called the Uniform Commercial Code ("UCC"). Louisiana didn't need it since their commercial law was already codified and other countries do not need it if they do not have federal and state (or their local equivalent of "state") laws as does the US. The UCC was adopted to provide standard rules specifically to facilitate interstate commerce. Without the UCC or something like it, different state rules could create a horrible problem of communication, misunderstanding and lawsuits.

In transactions or agreements regarding the sale of goods, we look to the UCC. For purposes of the UCC, "goods" are movable, tangible things. Securities (like stocks and bonds), real property (land and buildings) and contract rights are not "goods."

When a situation arises in which it is unclear whether a transaction is for personal services or for the sale of goods, courts have generally looked to the UCC and attempted to be consistent with the UCC even if the common law was the applicable body of law.

While detailed coverage of the UCC is beyond the scope of this book, it is helpful to know that it exists and to what it applies. You can consult an attorney for specific questions and purchase a copy of the UCC for reference.

2. Definition of a Contract

A "contract" is an agreement that has all of the elements described below. Practically all of us enter into a contract many times each week. Here are some examples:

> You go to a self-service gas station to fill up. You pay the cashier and he agrees to give you some gas. *That's a contract.*

> You go to the supermarket and bring some groceries to the check out. You pay for them and the market lets you take the groceries. *That's a contract, too.*

There are several types of contracts. It's not so important that you memorize the differences or the names; but it is important to remember that they are all contracts.

a. Express

An express agreement is a specific agreement between two or more parties. Although an express agreement can be oral or written, there is a doctrine called the "Statute of Frauds" (discussed below) that says that certain kinds of contracts <u>must</u> be "evidenced by a writing" to be enforceable, such as a contract involving real estate.

b. Implied-In-Fact

An agreement arising from the conduct of the parties rather than by words -- such as the supermarket example above -- is called a contract that is implied-in-fact.

c. Implied-In-Law

Even if two parties did not directly agree to anything, the law doesn't like seeing one party take advantage of another. For instance, one of the elements discussed below is *capacity*; meaning a person under the age of 18 who enters into a contract can *disavow* that contract and not be liable for it.

Assume a painter came to John's 16 year old son, Juan, and offered to paint their fence for $100. Juan agrees. John hears this, knows Juan is 16 and figures he'll be able to get out of paying because Juan can void the contract. This is a situation where John knowingly receives the benefits of the contract after he could have stopped the deal before the painter had done anything. If the painter can prove John heard the initial conversation with Juan, the courts will allow the painter to recover. (The tough part for the painter, however, is proving John heard the deal in the first place.)

d.   Bilateral

A bilateral contract is an agreement in which a promise for future performance is given in exchange for a promise for future performance. For example, "I promise to do something if you promise to pay me when I do it."

e.   Unilateral

A unilateral contract is an agreement in which a promise for future performance is given in exchange for an act or forbearance to act. For example: (1) "If you drive me to work I'll give you $1." (2) "If you don't smoke today I'll give you $5." In these cases, the second party didn't promise to do anything; but if he/she does drive the first person to work or not smoke today, the first party will pay them.

f.   Executory

An executory contract is one which has not yet been performed; only promises given. When an executory contract has been completed, it has been "executed."

g.   Unconscionable

An unconscionable agreement is one in which the terms are so one-sided that no reasonable person would have agreed to them if there weren't unreasonable pressure to do so.

For example: A person who has been walking in the desert for 3 days and has lost his wallet makes his way to a diner and asks for some food, promising to pay later. The owner says he'll provide a sandwich for $100 that is on the menu for $5. The starving person agrees and gets the sandwich. If the starving person later refuses to pay and the farmer sues him, the court will not make the person pay $100 because he agreed to pay $100 under extreme circumstances and pressure. It's a situation that you can look at and you could say, "That's just not right."

h.   Void

A void agreement is one which lacks one or more of the necessary elements of a contract (discussed, see below). No legal obligations have been created and there never was a valid contract.

i.   Voidable

Unlike a void agreement, voidable agreements are legally binding ones that can be made not binding; such as an agreement with a minor (see Capacity, below) or an agreement that says the parties can void it under certain circumstances.

j.   Unenforceable

An agreement may be unenforceable in a court of law because, for instance, one of the parties waited too long to bring it to court or the Statute of Frauds required it to be in writing.

Any contract can be a combination of the above. For instance, an agreement between Alice and Nick that Alice will do some tax planning for Nick and Nick will pay Alice $75 per hour is (1) express, (2) bilateral and (3) executory.

3.   Elements of a Contract

If the discussion above were the whole story, we could cut way down on legal fees; but, alas, no such luck. The following elements must all be present for a contract to be legally enforceable.

a.   Offer

There first must be an "offer." The person making the offer is the "offeror" and the person receiving the offer is the "offeree."

(1) What is an offer?

An offer is any communication that is specific enough to clearly show the intent to enter into a contract. The offer must be specific as to who the parties are, what is to be done, when and for what price.

Here are some examples of offers:

> Joe says to Bill, "I'll give you $50 for the coat you're wearing." Unless otherwise agreed, it is presumed that the cash will be paid when the coat is handed over.

> Bob's Auto Dealership advertises a car for the "low, low" price of $1999 and shows the license plate number. The reason those plates are so ridiculously big on TV commercials is that the dealer wants to make sure the price he's telling you about is only for that specific car, not all cars like that on the lot. Note that the commercials usually indicate something like "All cars subject to prior sale." The object here is to get you into the dealership because of low prices on specific cars.

> Jill says to Sherry, "I'll give you $1 to go to the store and pick up a quart of milk." The fact that Jill didn't specify regular, low fat or non-fat will not affect the validity of this offer.

Here are some examples that are not offers good enough to create a contract:

The local department store places the following advertisement: "New summer jackets for $1.00." Which jackets? To be a valid offer it would have to be something like "New summer jackets – style 123 from designer Joe Joe – for $1.00."

"I'm thinking about selling my car for about $2,000." The intent isn't clear, the time isn't clear and the price isn't definite. To be a valid offer it would have to be something like "I will sell you my car for $2,000 today."

"Would you pay me $20 if I jump off that bridge?" Even if the answer is "yes," the question was hypothetical and the person never said he would jump off that bridge. To be a valid offer it would have to be something like "I will jump off that bridge if you pay me $20."

In the case of sales of goods, the UCC gives considerably more latitude in the creation of a contract by creating a number of presumptions including the following:

- If no price is stated, it's a reasonable price.
- If no place of delivery is stated, it's seller's place of business.
- If no time for delivery is stated, it's within a reasonable time.

(2) When is an offer effective?

An offer is effective when it reaches the offeree. If you mail it, it's effective when received. If you tell someone the offer, it's effective right away. If you advertise it, it's effective when the viewer sees or hears it.

An offer is valid for as long as the offer states or, if no deadline is stated, for a *reasonable* time. ("Reasonable" is a standard used commonly throughout the law. It is not exact, but it allows the court to take into account all the circumstances and facts that may impact a person's judgment.)

An offer is effective only for the person to whom it was intended. For example, I mail an offer to you to sell my car for $2000 and your roommate sees the letter. Your roommate cannot accept my offer to you. Your roommate can, however, make his/her own offer to me to purchase my car for $2000.

(3) Revocation of an Offer

Except as described below, an offer can be revoked so long as such revocation is communicated to the offeree PRIOR TO "ACCEPTANCE" (see Acceptance). Revocation can be communicated to the offeree by any means no less effective than the way the original offer was communicated. For instance, if you communicated the offer by letter, you could revoke the offer by letter but not by advertisement in the local newspaper.

The EXCEPTIONS to the revocability rule stated above are:

(a) Options: An "option" is an agreement to hold an offer open for a specified period of time (90 days, for instance) and is, therefore, irrevocable during that period. The optionor (who is also the offeree) must have paid or given something to the offeror (see Consideration below).

(b) Certain sales of goods: Under the UCC, an offer is irrevocable without the offeree having given the offeror anything if (a) the offeror is a merchant in the type of goods being offered, (b) the offer was in writing and (c) the merchant gave assurance the offer would be held open for a period of time not to exceed 3 months.

Example: A telephone equipment manufacturer gives you a written bid and says he'll hold the offer open for 30 days. Under common law, the offer could be revoked any time prior to your acceptance of that offer. Under the UCC, however, the merchant cannot revoke this offer.

(4) Termination of an Offer

An offer is automatically terminated by operation of law upon:

    (a) the death or insanity of the either the offeror or offeree, except in the case of an option;

    (b) the death or destruction of the subject matter (the subject matter might be alive, such as livestock);

    (c) passage of a law, rule or regulation that would make the contract illegal;

    (d) passage of the time stated in the offer or, if none is stated, after a reasonable time.

b.   Acceptance

When an offeree receives an offer, he/she can respond or ignore it. If the offer is ignored, it will lapse by passage of time. If the offeree responds, he/she can either accept the offer, reject it, counter-offer or make an inquiry. Knowing the difference between a rejection, a counter-offer and an inquiry can sometimes be tricky; and it's an important difference since a rejection or counter-offer (which is, essentially, a rejection and a new offer) terminates the original offer while an "inquiry" keeps the offer open.

Why is that important to you? Because if you've rejected the original offer (or someone rejects yours) and they come back and later say, "Ok, I'll accept your original offer" you are not bound to it and could say "I changed my mind" with no legal liability.

(1) What is an acceptance?

    (a) If the offer was unilateral, acceptance is by the act or forbearance that was requested.

Example: "I will give you $1 to go to the store for some milk this afternoon." You accept by going; and although you have not completed your mission, I cannot take back my offer once you have started. There's no way you can breach this agreement, since you haven't accepted until you complete your mission and once you complete your mission you've done everything needed to satisfy the contract.

      (b)   If the offer was bilateral, acceptance is by promising to do what is asked.

Example: "I'll give you $1 if you promise to go to the store for some milk this afternoon." Unlike the previous example, now that you've promised to go to the store this afternoon, if you do not go you will have breached our agreement.

      (c)   Acceptance can be only by the person to whom the offer was made. Remember the earlier example about your roommate seeing my offer to sell you my car? Your roommate cannot accept even if you give him /her the letter voluntarily.

      (d)   As discussed above, acceptance of contracts covered by covered by common law must be exactly the same as the offer was. Under the UCC, however, an acceptance which contains additional terms can still be a valid acceptance (this requires more detail than covered in this book, so remember this is one of the things where a question should be asked).

      (e)   Generally, silence is not acceptance. However, if the parties have had previous dealings such that silence leads the offeror to believe there is acceptance, then the offer can be accepted by silence and the offeree held responsible for the contract, whether or not acceptance was intended.

      (f)   Unlike an offer which is effective when received by the offeree, acceptance of an offer is effective when it is sent if sent by the same means as the offer was communicated or by any other reasonable means.

Example: On January 1, I write you a letter offering to sell you my car for $2000. (I am not, by the way a merchant in cars.) You receive the letter on January 4. On January 5, I mail you a letter revoking my offer. On January 6, you mail me a letter accepting my offer. On January 7, you get my revocation. On January 9, I receive your acceptance.

There is binding agreement because:

1. My offer was effective *when you received it* on January 4.

2. Your acceptance was effective *when you mailed it* on January 6.

3. I could revoke this offer any time prior to your acceptance, but my revocation is not effective *until you receive it* on January 7, the day after your acceptance was effective.

Now add one more letter:

On January 8, you change your mind and want to revoke your acceptance.

If you communicate this to me before I receive your letter of acceptance, there will be no contract; but if I get your acceptance before your "change of mind" letter I can hold you to the contract.

    (2)   What is a rejection?

        (a)   As mentioned above, failure to respond is usually a rejection; unless the parties have a history or pattern of dealings in which silence IS acceptance.

        (b)   Words or conduct that indicate rejection are sufficient.

        (c)   A purported acceptance where I change your offer in any way is a counter-offer; which is a rejection. *An inquiry, however, is not a rejection.*

Example: You offer to perform certain services for me for $2000. I say, "OK, but I'll have to pay you in 30 days." You didn't mention any specific terms; therefore it's presumed you meant all cash at the time the services are performed. Although I seemed to accept your offer, I changed the terms of payment; which serves as a rejection and counter-offer. Your offer is no longer effective and I've made a new offer to you: Namely, I will pay you $2000 in 30 days if you perform certain services for me. It's now up to you to accept or reject the counter-offer.

Example: You offer to sell me your car for $2000 (and you're not a merchant). I know that's a good deal but figure I'll negotiate so I say, "No, I'll give you $1500." If you say "no" to that and I then agree to take the car for $2000, you could say, "Forget it" and have no obligation to me. When I rejected your offer, the offer was terminated.

AN INQUIRY, HOWEVER, WOULD HAVE KEPT THE OFFER ALIVE.

If, after you offered to sell me your car for $2,000, I said, "That price seems a little high. Would you consider $1500?" the offer would still be open since I did not say I wouldn't pay $2000. I simply asked if you'd take less. That small difference in language and attitude could make an enormous difference.

Under the UCC (sales of goods by merchants) there are some differences as compared to the common law rules. Under the UCC, offers by merchants of the goods being sold can be accepted where the acceptance includes *additional* terms. (Note that the above example with the car does not come under the UCC because the offeror was not a merchant in cars and even if the UCC did apply, the purported acceptance included a *change* of terms not *additional* terms, so the response would still be a counter-offer.)

Where the offeror is a merchant and the offeree is not, an acceptance is valid even if it contains additional terms, which terms can be accepted or rejected by the offeror. The offeror cannot, however, take back his offer by saying the offer was rejected.

> Example: I'm in the business of selling TV's and you want to buy one. I offer to sell it to you at the very special price of just $300. You say "I accept. Deliver it to my home as soon as you can." Since I never said anything about delivery, it's presumed you're going to take it from my store. I can say "no" to delivering it, but I cannot retract my offer to sell you the TV for $300.

If both offeror and offeree are merchants, the additional terms automatically become part of the agreement unless:

> (a) the new terms *materially alter* the offer, or
> (b) the offeror gives written notification of his objection to the new terms within a reasonable time, or
> (c) the offer expressly precludes additional terms.

c.   Consideration

(1) "Consideration" is getting something you weren't *entitled to* before (meaning you're getting a "legal benefit") or giving something you didn't have to give before (a "legal detriment"). Consideration can be money, property, doing something or not doing something.

(2) Generally, courts do not care about the fairness of the exchange, except in the case of unconscionable contracts (described above).

> Example: You agree to give me your car in exchange for my pen. As long as you're over 18 and not mentally impaired by illness or duress, the court will enforce this contract.

4.   Statute of Frauds

As described above, contracts can be oral. However, the Statute of Frauds provides that some kinds of contracts <u>must</u> be *evidenced by a writing* to be enforceable. This does not always mean the contract must be in writing; only that there must be something in writing to support the existence of that agreement. The difficulty, even if no writing is required, is proving the terms of the oral agreement; so keep that in mind when making an oral agreement.

Contracts which are subject to the Statute of Frauds are:

a.   Guarantees

Guarantees are promises to be responsible for the debts of another if the other person doesn't pay. There is an exception to the writing requirement if the guarantor has something important to gain by guaranteeing the agreement.

Examples:

Joe promises to pay his brother's debt if the brother doesn't pay. This promise must be evidenced by a writing.

Joe promises to pay the debt of his corporation if his corporation defaults; and without Joe's guarantee the credit will not be extended to Joe's corporation. Since Joe is getting a material benefit out of this transaction, there is no writing required for the promise to be enforceable.

b.   Contracts for the sale or transfer of interests in land

(1) Any sale of land or rights to land

(2) Leases that last longer than 1 year

c.   Contracts that cannot be performed within 1 year from the date of making

Example:

"I promise to pay you to work for me for 2 years" is unenforceable unless in writing.

"I promise to pay you to work for me as long as you live" need not be in writing since you could die within 1 year. Therefore, the contract is *capable* (regardless how likely) of being performed within 1 year from the date of mailing.

"I promise to pay you to work for me for 1 year starting next week" is not enforceable without a writing since full completion of the contract from the date the contract is made is 1 year and 1 week.

d.   Sales for goods for more than $500.

Exceptions are:

(1) As between merchants, a written confirmation of an order from one to the other must be objected to within 10 days from receipt of the confirmation or be bound by it.

(2) If a portion of the goods have been paid for, there is no need for a writing to enforce the whole contract.

(3) If the party who is trying to avoid the contract admits in court that such an agreement for the sale of goods was made, no additional writing is needed.

(4) If the goods to be purchased were to be specially manufactured for the purchaser, the goods are not resellable in the normal course of the seller's business and the seller had made a substantial start in their manufacture, no writing is needed.

5.   Reality of Consent

In some cases you can have all the foregoing elements of a contract, but some other factors make the contract *voidable*.

a.   Fraud

In order for a party to be able to void a contract based on fraud, all of the following must exist:

(1) There was a *misrepresentation of a material fact which substantially influenced the decision of a reasonable person.*

    (a) A flat out lie is an easy misrepresentation.

    (b) An opinion is not a misrepresentation of fact unless it's the opinion of an "expert."

    (c) Silence or failure to tell someone of a known problem can be a misrepresentation if one party knows of a defect that the other party cannot readily detect or one party has a fiduciary duty to the other.

(2) One party has the *intent to deceive* the other.

(3) The injured party *justifiably relied* on the misrepresentation.

(4) The injured party must have *damages*.

The potential remedies in the case of fraud are:

Rescission: Undue the contract and put the parties in as much as possible the same position as they would have been had the contract never been entered into.

Compensatory damages: Pay the damaged party the amount of money to cover his actual costs resulting from the fraud.

Consequential damages: Pay the damaged party the amount of money to cover his lost profits, maybe loss of goodwill or other elements that happened as a consequence of the fraud.

Punitive damages: Pay the damaged party and amount the court deems appropriate to punish the party committing the fraud, unrelated to the actual damages and costs sustained by the damaged party.

b.   Innocent Misrepresentation

The elements of this are the same as fraud except there is *no intent to deceive*. The only remedy available here is rescission.

c.   Mistake

(1) If only one party made a mistake (unilateral), there is generally no relief unless the other party knew or should have known of this mistake.

Example: You walk into my antique shop and see an item that you think is a cabinet worth $20,000 and offer me $10,000, thinking you'll negotiate me down. I paid $3000 and eagerly accept $8000. After taking the cabinet to your insurance appraiser, he tells you the cabinet is worth $5000. You could not void this contract.

(2) If both parties made a mistake as to the same material fact, the contract may be rescinded by either party.

d.   Duress

Duress is caused by acts or threats of violence against a person or his property which deprives the person of his/her free will. The remedy is rescission.

e.   Undue influence

Undue influence is mental coercion which prevents the use of free will. The remedy is rescission.

6. Rights of third parties

a.   Third party beneficiaries

In some cases, a person who is not a party to the contract has rights because the contract was for his/her benefit.

Rather than go into detail on this issue or even give an example which might be too narrow to give a complete picture, we'll leave this as an issue for future materials. Just remember that even if you are not a party to a contract between two other parties, if that contract benefitted you, you may have some rights even though you are not a party.

b.   Assignment and delegation

A contract entails both rights and duties. A transfer of rights is an assignment; while a transfer of duties is a delegation. Whether a party can assign or delegate depends on the contract and nature of the rights and duties to be transferred.

> Example: If I have a right to the payment of money from Julia for services I already performed, I can assign that right to you.
>
> On the other hand, if I have not yet performed the services to Julia and assignment of payment to you may jeopardize the quality of my services to Julia (since I'm not getting anything out of it), I may be prevented from making such an assignment.

I cannot delegate duties not yet performed to someone else if they are personal in nature and you hired me because of my unique skills and ability. In fact, many contracts expressly prohibit assignment or delegation without permission of the other party to the contract.

A delegation of duties under a contract (which is an assumption of the duties by the new party) does not relieve the original party of his/her responsibility under the contract. If you delegate duties to someone and the new person causes damage, you can be held liable. If the parties intend the transferring party to be totally absolved of all future responsibility, they must enter into a *novation* (essentially, a whole new deal), which is the complete substitution of one party for another.

> Example: You hire Joe to do a two-week job. After the first week, Joe says he has a great opportunity elsewhere and his pal Ed will finish the job. You agree and Ed makes a mess. You can hold Joe liable.

> If Joe wanted out completely, the agreement would have had to specifically include a release of Joe from his obligations under the original contract. This is called a *novation*.

7.   **Common law remedies**

a.   Money damages

   (1)   *Nominal damages* are more symbolic than anything else. An award of, for example, $1 says to the plaintiff "you're right but you weren't hurt."

   (2)   *Compensatory damages* are intended to compensate the aggrieved party for his or her loss. Figure what you're out because of the other party's acts or omissions, and that's the amount of the compensatory damages you can ask for. Lost profits are not included in compensatory damages. For example, if someone starts a fire in your shop destroying everything inside which cost you $10,000 and which you would have sold for $20,000, only your $10,000 cost is included in compensatory damages.

   (3)   *Consequential damages* are where you might be able to get lost profits but only where the other party had specific knowledge of the consequences of his/her acts or omissions.

   (4)   *Quantum meruit* means "fair value." This is one way the court uses to determine how much damages are fair if there is no more precise way to figure the damages. For instance, in the earlier example about the painted fence, the court

might find that John can't be held to the price stated by the painter to Juan, but that it would be unfair to not give the painter anything since John <u>did</u> get the value of a newly fence. This would be a case for "quantum meruit" or giving the painter the fair value of his work.

(5) *Punitive damages* are not recoverable in contract actions. However, in a case where the other party did something wrong, there may also be an action in *tort* for willful misconduct or negligence. A simple case of not living up to a deal does not give rise to punitive damages.

(6) *Liquidated damages* are put into contracts at the time the contract is created because figuring out the damages later would be too difficult. Often you'll see a deposit being kept by the party who received the deposit as *liquidated damages* in the event of breach by the other party. The law hates, however, *forfeitures*. So, if it looks like the amount is totally out of line, the court may declare the so-called "liquidated damages" a forfeiture and strike them down, returning the money to the other party.

b.   Specific performance

Specific performance is granted to enforce the terms of a contract in cases where money damages would not be sufficient. For instance, each piece of real estate or original art is unique. If you had already paid your money and the seller just decided not to sell, getting your money back may not be sufficient since you can't just go buy the same item somewhere else. This is a case where specific performance could be awarded.

c.   Rescission

Rescission is where everything is put back as if the contract had never been entered into. In the example in the preceding paragraph, if you could get your money back and go buy the same item elsewhere for the same price, getting your money back would, assuming it all happened in a short period of time, put you in the same position as if you had never entered into the first agreement.

d.   Mitigation of damages

Mitigation of damages is required of someone who has been hurt by the breach of a contract. This means you, as the aggrieved party, have an obligation to try to minimize your damages.

Example: You own a building and a tenant breaks the lease. You have an obligation to try to get someone else to rent that space at market value and not just let it sit unoccupied expecting the old tenant to pay you.

8.   Risk of loss under the UCC

If your business involves buying or selling goods, the issue of who has the risk of loss is critical.

Example: You manufacture 10,000 widgets and sell them to a buyer in another country. On the way, the truck that's carrying those widgets catches fire and all the widgets are destroyed. Does the buyer still have to pay? That depends on who bears the risk of loss.

The allocation of risk of loss has nothing to do with who owns the goods at the time they're lost, damaged or destroyed. The UCC allows the parties to specifically agree and, in the absence of such agreement, provides as follows.

1. If one party is in breach, the breaching party bears the risk of loss.

2. If the terms of the shipment are "FOB" ("Free on Board"), the risk of loss passes from seller to buyer at the place at which the shipment is FOB.

Examples:

"FOB destination" means the seller bears the risk of loss until the goods reach their destination.

"FOB seller's warehouse" means buyer assumes the risk of loss as soon as the goods leave the seller's warehouse.

"FOB carrier" means the buyer assumes the risk of loss as soon the goods reach the shipper that will take the goods from the seller to the buyer.

3. If the seller is a merchant, the seller has the risk of loss until buyer receives the goods, *unless otherwise agreed* ... meaning that if you are the seller and you want to reduce your risk you could negotiate that the sale is, for example, FOB seller's warehouse and the risk then passes to the buyer as soon as the goods leave your warehouse.

4. If the seller is not a merchant, then the seller has the risk of loss until the goods are tendered to the buyer, *unless otherwise agreed*. This means that as soon as seller makes the goods reasonably available to buyer, buyer assumes the risk.

5. *Sale on Approval* is when goods are delivered primarily for personal use, such as products you have delivered from an online seller. The seller retains full risk of loss until the goods are accepted and must accept return of the goods even if they are exactly what the buyer ordered. In this case, "acceptance" is presumed if buyer does not return the goods in the prescribed manner and within the prescribed time period.

6. *Sale or Return* is when the buyer receives goods primarily for resale, and simply has the right to return the goods under stated conditions, if any. In this case, the buyer has full risk of loss until the goods are received back by the seller.

9. Remedies for breach under the UCC

If a buyer orders goods from a seller who ships the wrong things, such goods are called *non-conforming*. A non-conformity can be in the model, size, color, style or quantity.

a.   If a seller breaches by delivering goods which do not conform to what the buyer ordered, the buyer may:

    (1) accept the whole order, or

    (2) reject the whole order, or

    (3) accept part and reject part, or

    (4) *cover* by purchasing substitute goods elsewhere and getting reimbursed for any additional price paid for such substitute goods.

Example: You have a contract to buy widgets from ABC Co. for $2.00 each to be delivered in 30 days; and ABC defaults (meaning they don't deliver on time). You go to XYZ Co. to buy the same widgets and you have to pay $2.50. You would be entitled to $.50 for each widget you buy from XYZ up to the total originally contracted for with ABC. (Of course, if your contract with ABC didn't provide that you get your legal and attorneys' fees, you could end up spending more than you'd get back. So, always consider the practical implications of enforcing your rights.)

Note that a buyer has the right to inspect goods received prior to acceptance <u>except</u> if the goods are shipped COD ("Cash On Delivery"), in which case the buyer must accept or reject *without inspection*.

Notwithstanding a seller's breach, the buyer has a duty to be specific about the non-conformity(s). Seller then has a right to "cure" the non-conformity under specific provisions of the UCC.

b.   If a buyer breaches, the seller may:

(1) prior to buyer's receipt of the goods, resell the goods through public or private sale and recover any loss in the price received from buyer, or

(2) stop the shipment if the buyer is insolvent, or

(3) recover goods received by an insolvent buyer if demand is made within 10 days of receipt.

10. Bulk sales

The sale or transfer of property of the business which is *not in the ordinary course of seller's business* is improper unless proper notice is provided to creditors. Failure to comply with appropriate procedures will permit creditors of the seller to enforce their claims against the purchasers of the sold property.

11. Warranties

a. What is a "warranty"?

(1) An *express warranty* is when a seller states a fact (not opinion) which is part of the reason why buyer makes the purchase even if the seller never uses the words "warranty" or "guarantee."

(2) An *implied warranty* is when the law imposes certain warranties that apply without being stated by the seller.

(a) An *implied warranty of merchantability* applies to the sale of goods by a merchant seller and says that all goods sold shall be fit for the *ordinary purpose* for which they were intended.

Example: You buy an electric drill. The first time you use the drill it overheats and catches fire. When you bring it back to the dealer he tells you neither they nor the manufacturer ever warranted the drill against catching fire.

Regardless of what was not said, an electric drill is not supposed to catch fire under normal use and the law implies a warranty of *merchantability*. The buyer will be able to get a refund or a new drill or, if there were any damages caused by the defective drill, money for that, too.

(b) An *implied warranty of fitness for a particular purpose* covers sales of goods by both merchant and non-merchant sellers and applies to a situation where the seller knows the buyer's particular purpose or use for the goods and the buyer relies on the seller's skill and judgment in selecting or purchasing the goods.

Example: You go into a hardware store to buy a drill and you tell the dealer you want it for concrete, something for which most drills are not made. The dealer recommends a particular drill and you buy it in reliance on the dealer's recommendation ... and it overheats, catching fire.

When you bring it back, the sales manager says that the model you bought isn't supposed to be used on concrete. However, you reasonably relied on the recommendation of someone who knew the particular purpose for the drill and supposedly had the expertise to make such a recommendation. In this case, the law implies a warrant of fitness for particular purpose. [The difficulty will be proving the seller knew the particular purpose.]

(3) A *warranty of title* is when the seller warrants he has clear ownership of the goods sold. The only way for a seller to avoid this warranty is to expressly state that the goods are being sold *subject to* someone else's interest or lien. Surprises such as finding out someone has a lien on goods was largely ended when states started recording such liens, making it possible for anyone to look up in county records

what liens exist on major items of property such as equipment, cars or, of course, real estate.

b.   Disclaimers – If you are a seller, disclaimers are how you avoid liability for certain things. A good example is when you hear or see an advertisement for a medicine and a good portion of the ad is taken up with all the side effects and warnings. Those are the disclaimers for that product; meaning that if one of those things happen, the manufacturer/seller will not be liable.

   (1) For Implied Warranties

      (a) Merchantability: The disclaimer does not have to be in writing but if it is it must be clear and conspicuous.

      (b) Fitness for Particular Purpose: The disclaimer must be in writing.

   (2) If the buyer has had an opportunity to inspect the goods, there are no warranties for reasonably discoverable defects.

B.   AGENCY

1.   Definition

a.   What is an *agency*?

   (1) *Agency* is the relationship where one person represents another. The person being represented is the *principal* and the representative is the *agent*. Employees and others can act as agents.

   (2) Contracts created by the agent are between the principal and a third party.

   (3) It is presumed that the principal has any relevant information the agent has. In the other words, the principal can't use "I didn't know" or "He didn't tell me" as a valid defense in an action by the third party on a contract created by the agent.

Example: A lease requires that cancellation can be effective with at least after 30 days' notice. If you are the tenant and you give notice to the landlord's agent that you are ending the lease, you will have satisfied the notice requirement 30 days from when you gave notice, irrespective of when the agent gives the notice to the landlord.

b.   What is an *independent contractor*?

A person you hire to do a job for you may be an *independent contractor*. The distinction between an agent and an independent contractor is critical because of the powers and duties an agent has with respect to the principal.

An independent contractor is someone who works for him or herself and is hired to perform a service with certain intended results. The person hiring the independent contractor does not control or direct the way the results are generated.

An independent contractor does not have the special powers that an agent has, as described below; but neither does he/she have the responsibility to the employer that an agent does.

Examples:

You call a plumber to come fix your sink. You might watch or tell the plumber to come at a certain time or tell the plumber to not put his tools on the table, but you are not directing the actual work. After all, if you could direct the work you probably could have done the repair yourself. The plumber is an independent contractor.

You hire a salesperson who handles other companies' products as well as yours. You hired him on the basis of how he does his job, but beyond that you don't tell him how to run his life or business. However, the more conditions you impose and more control you have, the closer you come to an agency relationship. Why is it important that this outside salesperson not be an agent? Because if he were an agent (including an employee) you could be bound by deals, concessions and quotations he makes without consulting you.

2. Fiduciary duty

a.   Fiduciary Duties

Fiduciary duty is the duty to act on behalf of someone else with the highest possible degree of trust and loyalty.

An agent must not use any information or property acquired through the agency relationship for the agent's personal benefit without permission of the principal.

An agent must not act for more than one principal at a time *without the principal's permission, prior agreement* or *industry custom.*

> Example: No one expects a real estate agent to work for only 1 principal (owner) at a time.

An agent must not divulge confidential information obtained through the agency relationship, whether or not for the agent's benefit, without permission of the principal.

An agent must not mix the principal's money with his/her own (called *commingling*). An agent must be able to account for all the principal's funds at all times.

3. Creation of an agency

a. Agency Creation

(1) An agency can be created by express agreement; although no writing is required except in the case of real estate agents.

(2) An agency can be created by ratification. This is where someone does or says something on your behalf without your approval; but you then accept the benefit of what that someone did or said. This acceptance can be by words or conduct.

Example: John negotiated a contract with a customer on behalf of Susan's company. John never asked Susan if he could do this; he just did it. Susan was surprised, but liked the contract and started to perform under it. By accepting the benefits of the contract, Susan *ratified* the agency between John and Susan. She could have said, "I accept the contract and you as an agent" to John; although simply performing under the contract was enough.

(3) An agency can be created by *estoppel*. Notice that the Latin term "estoppel" contains the word "stop." The legal application of estoppel means that someone is stopped from making a certain argument. A principal may be *estopped* from denying there was an agency because the principal's conduct led some third party to *justifiably rely* on the existence of the agency relationship.

Example: Sherry, Susan and Joan are sitting at lunch. Sherry is an actress, Susan is a talent agent and Joan is a television producer. Susan tells Joan that Sherry will work on Joan's television program for $1000 per show. Susan is not, in fact, Sherry's agent but Joan doesn't know that and Sherry, who's sitting right there listening to all this, doesn't say anything. When Joan agrees, Sherry would technically be obligated under the terms of whatever agreement Susan had just negotiated.

The practical issue in this case as it is in any case where something happens verbally rather than in writing is one of proof. Sherry and Susan could both either deny that any agreement was reached or that they were drunk or kidding and it was clear that no agency was intended.

4.   Authority

A principal will be held liable for the acts or statements of an agent *acting within his/her authority*. This is the key to an agency relationship and the difference between an agent and an independent contractor, who does not have this power.

How do you know if the proper authority exists?

a.   Actual authority

    (1) Actual authority can be created by an express agreement between the principal and agent. An oral agreement is fine unless the Statute of Frauds applies, as in the case of real estate agents and transactions.

    (2) Actual authority can also be implied based on the express authority.

        Example: You give your employee (who is also an *agent*) the express authority to travel on behalf of your business. The authority of that employee to obligate the business to pay for hotel rooms would be implied (reasonably assumed) based on the express authority to travel.

        In a case such as this where implied authority is based on express authority, the principal and agent most likely intended it anyways, but just did not spell it out.

    (3) Express authority can also be created by ratification, as described earlier.

b.   Apparent or ostensible authority

Apparent or *ostensible authority* is a very important category because it is in this area that most disputes arise. One person commits the business to something, the business later denies it and the person to whom the commitment was made says, "How was I supposed to know he didn't have the authority?" The business is stuck.

There are three requirements for apparent authority to exist:

(1) The conduct of the principal must make it appear that the agent had the appropriate authority. Remember that conduct can include silence.

(2) The party to whom the commitment was made must have *justifiably relied* on the appearance of proper authority. *Justifiable reliance* is determined by asking "Would a *reasonable* person be justified in relying on this?"

(3) The party to whom the commitment was made must have been damaged by reliance on the apparent authority. Otherwise, as they say in basketball, "No harm - No foul."

Examples:

You go into a car showroom and the sales manager gives you a written quote for a particular car. The sales manager knows you're going to sell your car to help pay for the new one. Based on the new car quote, you sell your old car that afternoon. When you go to pick up your new car, the general manager of the company tells you the sales manager didn't have the authority to give the kind of concessions he did and that the company would not honor the deal.

Your argument is: You dealt with the sales manager whose job it is to make these kinds of deals. If the company limits the sales manager's authority, there was nothing to indicate that to you. You did, in fact, suffer damage in *justifiable reliance* on the apparent authority of the sales manager because you sold your car

and now have no transportation without the new one...
Technically, you win. (You still may leave the dealership that day without your car.)

If the receptionist had given you the quote instead of the sales manager, there would not have been *justifiable* reliance on the receptionist's apparent authority to make you that deal.

A harder variation, though, is when the salesperson makes you the deal. The general manager might argue that consumers know that a salesperson must get deals approved by the sales manager. But is it the buyer's responsibility to make sure the salesperson did, in fact, get the deal approved? It probably depends on the circumstances and whether the salesperson did anything to suggest to you that he got the deal approved.

The moral of this story is that if you, as a principal, put special limitations on the powers of your agent that third parties are not aware of and which limitations your agent then violates, you can still be held liable under the contract with the third party. You would, however, have a right to recover any damages or costs you incur from the agent based on a claim of breach of contract or breach of fiduciary duty.

5. Liability of the agent

a. On contracts

Since the agent is not a party to the contract between the principal and a third party, the agent is generally not liable under any contract created by the agent. However, there are some instances where the agent can be held responsible.

If the agent represents the principal without telling the third party that he/she (the agent) is actually representing a principal, it appears to the third party that the agent is acting on his/her own behalf. Consequently, the third party is relying on the impressions of and relationship with the agent.

In this case, the third party can hold the agent liable. Even if the third party later learns of the existence and identify of the principal, the third party can still choose between the principal and agent who he (the third party) wants to hold responsible.

On the other side, a principal whose existence and identify are not known at the time the contract is entered into can often still hold the third party responsible under such contract.

b.   On torts

A "tort" is not a French pastry; it is a wrong that is done to someone or against someone's property. Examples of torts are assault, battery, slander, vandalism and theft. Some torts are done intentionally and some are done because of failure to use reasonable care ("negligence"). Although many torts are also crimes, the differences are:

(1) A criminal claim is brought in criminal court by the government. A tort claim is brought in civil court by the party (or his/her representative, as in a wrongful death action) who was hurt and wants something.

(2) A criminal action is brought for the purpose of punishing and/or rehabilitating the criminal (depending on your personal feelings about our criminal justice system). A tort action is brought for the purpose of recovering money, forcing someone to do something or stopping them from doing something.

Every person is liable for his or her own torts. Consequently, an agent cannot escape liability for his/her torts by saying he/she was acting on behalf of someone else.

The greater question is whether the principal is liable for torts of the agent. The answer is "yes" if the tort was committed within the agent's scope of authority. This is called *The Doctrine of Respondeat Superior* (the superior is responsible).

Examples:

John works at ABC Company where he is a salesperson. A customer comes in and asks for an item, which John locates behind some boxes. In the process of moving the boxes, John negligently knocks the customer down, breaking her foot.

The customer can recover against John or the ABC Company, since John was clearly acting within the scope of his authority when he was moving the boxes to get to the item the customer requested. If ABC were held liable, however, ABC would have a right to reimbursement (also called *indemnification*) from John. (Actually being able to get the money from John is an entirely different matter.)

Same example as above except a different customer comes in and says something bad about ABC Company. John then punches the customer.

Although John might say he was standing up for the company, he was not acting within the scope of his authority when he hit a customer. ABC would not be liable, though John certainly would. (As a practical matter, however, the customer would still sue ABC, which would call in its insurance company. Depending on the amount of the claim, the insurance company might just settle with the customer if the settlement would be less than the cost of going to court.)

The doctrine of respondeat superior may sound like just legal talk, but say your business offers delivery service. Every time you send a driver out, there is the possibility of getting into an accident and you might be responsible (depending on the circumstances). This is an example of how a legal principle can directly impact how you run your business by affecting whether or not you offer delivery and, if so, by who and at what cost. Is that service worth the additional insurance and other costs associated with that service?

6. Termination of an agency

a. Agency Termination

    (1) An agency relationship can be terminated in several ways:

        (a)   by expiration of an agreed period of time.

            Examples:

            "...at the end of 90 days from the date of this agreement."

            "...at midnight, June 30."

        (b)   by notice from the principal to the agent when no definite time period was agreed.

        (c)   by mutual agreement.

        (d)   by completing the task for which the agency was created.

        (e)   Upon the bankruptcy of the principal.

        (f)   Upon the death or insanity of either principal or agent.

    (2) Notice to third parties of the termination of an agency relationship is very important to the principal. Otherwise, the agent could still create binding contracts for the principal based on apparent authority. The principal should give two kinds of notices:

        (a)   Actual notice to third parties who have previously dealt with the agent.

        (b)   Constructive notice to others by publishing the termination in a newspaper of general circulation to the people who would otherwise rely on the apparent authority of the agent.

Obviously, this kind of termination is time consuming and expensive, especially if you had to do it every time an employee left. You don't.

In the case of outside salespeople, orders should state clearly that home office approval is required before the order is valid. As for employees inside your store or office, you need not worry about most because it would not be justifiable for a third party to rely on any claimed authority outside of the store or office.

C.   INTELLECTUAL PROPERTY

One of the most frightening thoughts in creating a new idea is that someone will steal it. Though most new business ideas are not protectable, the federal government has created various means of protecting ideas and products.

As I have said so many times, the goal of this book is not to make you an expert on anything, but rather to give you some basic knowledge so you will know where the issues might be.

Since patents, trademarks and copyrights are not physical property like a chair or building (though you may have a letter from the government saying that you have, for example, Patent #12345), these *ideas* are called *intellectual property*. The intricacies are extensive, but here is some very basic information that may help guide you to ask the right questions.

1.   Legal means are there to protect your intellectual property

a. Patents

A patent, like a copyright or trademark, gives the owner the exclusive right to use the covered material for a specified period of time.

A *patent* is given to protect a new *product*. It is issued by the US Patent & Trademark Office (USPTO). There are 6 kinds of patents but the two most common are:

A *utility patent* can be issued for a product that does something new or differently than it was done before including, under certain circumstances, unique methods of conducting business. According to the USPTO, approximately 90% of patents are utility patents.

A *design patent* can be issued for a product that looks different.

b. Copyrights

A *copyright* protects the visual presentation of an idea, such as a book or artwork. Copyrights are issued by the Copyright Office of the Library of Congress. This protection applies only to the specific presentation of the subject. For example, if you write a love story that takes place during World War II, only the text of your book can be protected - not the title and not the theme.

c. Trademarks

Trademarks are the names, logos and designs you see on every sign, letterhead and advertisement. Trademarks are the representation of the brands known all over the world ... or the ones that are still in your head. Like patents, trademarks are issued by the USPTO; but unlike patents, you can have a trademark without registering it with the USPTO which is called a *common law trademark*.

You can tell the difference between a *common law* trademark and a *registered* trademark by the symbol that appears with the mark. A common law trademark has the ™ whereas a registered trademark has the ®. It is a federal offense to use ® if your trademark is not registered.

You can get a common law trademark by using your mark with the ™. You can apply for a registered trademark through the USPTO; and until it is issued you can use ™.

In either case, the reason you want to protect your trademark -which represents your business and the goodwill you create - is so others cannot use your trademark to compete with you or to use your brand and goodwill you have built to their benefit.

The difference between the common law trademark and the registered trademark is the process of enforcement. In either case, the trademark owner that believes someone else is infringing on his/her trademark must prove to the court that he was using the trademark before the alleged infringer. That can be done for a common law trademark with dated advertising, websites, manuals, menus, etc.; but it might not be so clear and an infringer in a different state could argue that your brand has no goodwill in that state because no one had ever heard of it there before.

The advantages of a registered trademark is that the registration date issued by the USPTO shifts the burden to the infringer to show they were using the mark before that date and it is federal, so you can sue in a federal court and the *different state* argument does not work.

Trademarks can be created for words and for designs.

d. Trade Secrets

Trade secrets are ideas and information that you developed for your business that constitute an advantage for you, something without which your business might be hurt. Trade secrets could include a formula (for example, the secret formula for Coca Cola) or it could be your customer list or even something that you did not want to patent because in order to patent something you have to tell everyone how you made it (again, like Coca Cola).

e. Confidentiality Agreements

Confidentiality or *Non-disclosure Agreements* (also known as an "NDA") are contracts in which one party agrees to disclose certain information and ideas to someone and the other party agrees to keep that information and those ideas confidential; meaning not to tell anyone and not to use that information and those ideas for his or her own benefit. To put it bluntly, the other person agrees to not steal the idea and do it or tell someone else who might steal it.

You should always get an NDA signed before disclosing your idea to someone who is not already obligated to maintain your confidence, such as your attorney; and, in theory, NDA's are fine. As a practical matter, however, there are a number of issues and risks:

(1) If an NDA is too vague, most people will not sign it because it then could give you the opportunity to sue them based on something different than your idea.

Example: I ask you to sign an NDA that refers to "my idea for a new business," you sign it and I tell you about my idea for a new *widget*. You then invent a new *gadget* and I sue you saying my idea was for a gadget, not a widget company. You may win, but after spending money on defending the case. The trickier situation is where you had an idea for a widget and so did the other person, but it's either a different widget than yours or they had the idea for the same widget before you did. So, rather than risk an expensive lawsuit, the other people may simply not sign your NDA.

(2) How do you make an NDA not "too vague" so that someone else will sign it and a court will enforce it? Be more specific. The problem with being too specific is that the more you disclose in the NDA, the more of your idea you have revealed before the NDA is signed.

Example: I ask you to sign an NDA that refers to "my idea for a new widget that is made like this" and I give you all the specifications. After you have read the NDA, you know everything about my widget and you haven't signed the NDA, so when you make that widget yourself and I sue you, I have nothing to show I told you about that widget first.

(3) In all of the cases above, when you give someone an NDA, the only way it has any impact is if you are financially prepared (i.e., ready to spend money) to sue them if they violate the NDA. Still, having an NDA is much better than not having one.

2. How to protect yourself

a. Some basic steps for obtaining patents, trademarks and copyrights are outlined below. First, however, I want to talk "real world."

Even ideas that are protectable are not guaranteed protection. The reason is that a patent, trademark or copyright, while they are supposed to give you exclusive rights to that idea or products, are:

- limited to that specific idea, creating the opportunity for someone to start with your idea and make variations that avoid your patent or copyright;

- simply a right to sue the party violating your patent or copyright; and

- challengeable by anyone who argues the patent or copyright should not have been granted.

What good is that when you're up against a big company or anyone with a lot of money to spend on attorneys at a time when everything you've got is going to start a new business? The last thing you need is a major legal expense.

Since application for a patent requires disclosing the way a product is manufactured, it's not surprising that some major companies have chosen to not patent their products and relied on their internal abilities and mechanisms to protect their *trade secrets*. A good example of this is, as mentioned above, Coca Cola, which has never patented the formula for Coke because they'd have to disclose it.

b. So what's the answer?

Recognize that while most people have a great deal of integrity and are trustworthy, people look out for their own interests first.

On one hand, you don't want to be so paranoid that you never tell anyone about your idea; but, on the other hand, you don't want to make it too easy for others to steal your idea. Some people or companies will be tempted to take a good idea from you and claim it as their own.

Some of the following points may sound cynical and pessimistic, but it's a horrible feeling to see someone else making your idea work while you're sitting on the sidelines.

Do what you can under the rules but you really don't want to be involved in a legal action to enforce your patent or copyright – at least not until you are in the market and making money - and use a lot of common sense.

(1) Your best protection is to be the first and best in the marketplace. In this case, "best" doesn't necessarily refer to quality of your product or service, but rather to your marketing. Don't make a lot of noise until you're ready to open for business, otherwise you'll give others a lot of time to catch up.

(2) Your business plan should be based on a plan to get into the marketplace quickly and broadly once you've started.

(3) Don't talk to people you don't know about your idea unless there's a specific reason to. For instance, don't go into bars or restaurants and speak loudly about your great new idea. The wrong person may agree and do it himself.

(4) Don't talk to parties that could easily do your project themselves unless you're protected legally or are confident you can provide something they don't already have or can't easily duplicate. For instance, don't go to a widget manufacturer with an idea for a new widget unless you can bring expertise,

manpower or a patent that the manufacturer doesn't already have – and needs. I'm not assuming the manufacturer would steal your idea, but why take the chance when there are so many other avenues to go through.

(5) Use NDA's which at least establish that the party to whom you showed your idea expressly agreed to keep it confidential and to not use it to his advantage without you. The good news is that courts are particularly sensitive to the risk an individual bears when exposing his or her idea. The bad news is that even a confidentiality agreement will not protect you if the party to whom you showed your idea had come up with the same or similar idea independently of you. It would then be up to you to sue the company and force them to show all their developmental work.

c. Getting a Patent

The Office of Patents, Trademarks and Copyrights provides instructions for filing a patent application and there are many web sites and books to guide you.

While there is no requirement you use an attorney experienced in drafting patents, if you read some patents you will see that it appears to be somewhat of a different language. It is, in fact, a very specialized type of writing. I tried it once and it was a real learning experience. So, if you can afford it, get an attorney who specializes in writing patents (this is not something just any attorney can do well). You do not want to go through the trouble of filing a patent, disclosing your idea to the world, but doing it in a way that does not get you the protection you wanted or to which you might be entitled with a properly written patent application.

There is also a *provisional patent* which is simpler and enables you to get your idea on record so that if you file a full patent application within the prescribed time, the date of your application will be when you filed the *provisional* application. That may be just the protection you need while you are telling other people about your idea.

d. Getting a Trademark

An application form can be obtained from the Office of Patents, Trademarks and Copyrights or you can do it easily online. After completion of the application, payment of a fee and <u>approval</u> by the Office (which can take 9 months or more), your trademark is then "Registered" entitling you to use the ® designation. Use of the ® before approval – the *Notice of Allowance* -- by the USPTO is illegal.

The cost of registration can be a deterrent since there is a separate fee for each class of use.

> Example: Registration of your trademark for use on paper products is separate from registering that same mark for use on apparel. This is why you could register your trademark for calendars and see your trademark owned by someone else on blankets. The strategy might be to register the trademark in the primary class of use and also the class most susceptible to infringement and leave the other classes for your common law trademark protection. If someone else is using your registered trademark in a way that confuses the public to think the product or service is from you, then that is something you can stop regardless whether you have registered your mark in that classification.

e. Getting a Copyright

This process and law is similar to that of a trademark, enabling you to establish a copyright either by common law usage or by filing with the Library of Congress, and use of the © designation.

A handy trick for helping to establish (not all courts accept this) when you wrote something is to mail it to yourself in a sealed envelope by certified mail and leave it unopened until such time as you bring it out to show a court when you wrote your material.

In the case of written materials such as films or television scripts, the Writers Guild of America provides a registration service which accomplishes much the same as the mailing does above, by sealing your material in an envelope and maintaining a file of the sealed envelopes. You do not have to be a member of the Writers Guild to use their service.

VIII. CONCLUSION

Let's review what this book does not try to do:

- It does not give you *all the answers*.
- It does not tell you whether to be an entrepreneur.
- It does not tell you how to run your business.

What this book tries to do is give you some fundamental information to help you make better decisions and ask better questions.

If you encounter a situation or are faced with a problem and you remember reading something about it here that moves you toward finding a solution, this book will have served its purpose. You may have avoided a situation that could have proven very damaging to yourself, your family and your business.

And, so, if you want to be an entrepreneur, I wish you luck, good fortune and the satisfaction of achieving your dreams.

<u>NOTES</u>

NOTES

Made in the USA
Charleston, SC
20 February 2016